CONTEMPORARY WRITERS

BOOKS BY VIRGINIA WOOLF

The Voyage Out, 1915
Night and Day, 1919
Kew Gardens, 1919
Monday or Tuesday, 1921
Jacob's Room, 1922
The Common Reader: First Series, 1925
Mrs. Dalloway, 1925
To the Lighthouse, 1927
Orlando, 1928
A Room of One's Own, 1929
The Waves, 1931
Letter to a Young Poet, 1932
The Second Common Reader, 1932
Flush, 1933
The Years, 1937
Three Guineas, 1938
Roger Fry: A Biography, 1940
Between the Acts, 1941
The Death of the Moth and Other Essays, 1942
A Haunted House and Other Short Stories, 1944
The Moment and Other Essays, 1947
The Captain's Death Bed and Other Essays, 1950
A Writer's Diary, 1954
Virginia Woolf and Lytton Strachey: Letters, 1956
Granite and Rainbow, 1958
Contemporary Writers, 1965
Collected Essays (*4 vols.*), 1967
Mrs. Dalloway's Party, 1973
The Letters of Virginia Woolf. Vol. I: 1888–1912, 1975
Freshwater, 1976

CONTEMPORARY WRITERS

By Virginia Woolf

With a Preface by JEAN GUIGUET

A HARVEST BOOK

Harcourt Brace Jovanovich

NEW YORK AND LONDON

Printed in the United States of America

Library of Congress Cataloging in Publication Data

Woolf, Virginia Stephen, 1882–1941.
Contemporary writers.

(A Harvest book ; HB 347)
1. English fiction—History and criticism—Addresses, essays, lectures.
2. Criticism—Addresses, essays, lectures.
I. Title.
PR6045.072A16   1976   823'.9'1209   76-14984
ISBN 0-15-621450-4

First Harvest edition 1976

ABCDEFGHIJ

CONTENTS

Preface   7

PART ONE

The Claim of the Living   15
Caution and Criticism   18
In a Library   21
Women Novelists   24
A Man with a View   28
The Way of All Flesh   33

PART TWO

Journeys in Spain   39
The Sentimental Traveller   42
The Inward Light   44
One Immortality   47
A Room with a View   49
The Park Wall   51
Before Midnight   54
South Wind   56
Books and Persons   60
Mr Galsworthy's Novel   63
Philosophy in Fiction   67
The Green Mirror   71
Moments of Vision   74
Mr Merrick's Novels   77
The "Movie" Novel   82
Sylvia and Michael   85
War in the Village   87
The Rights of Youth   90

6 CONTENTS

Mr Hudson's Childhood 94
Honest Fiction 99
September 102
The Three Black Pennys 105
Java Head 108
Gold and Iron 111
The Pursuit of Beauty 113
Pleasant Stories 115
Mummery 117
The Tunnel 120
Romance and the Heart 123
The Obstinate Lady 126
Mr Norris's Method 128
Mr Norris's Standard 131
A Real American 135
Sonia Married 138
Winged Phrases 141
A Born Writer 146
Cleverness and Youth 149
Freudian Fiction 152
Revolution 155
Postscript or Prelude? 158

PREFACE

THE object of this book is to bring together Virginia Woolf's essays or reviews in which she dealt with contemporary fiction. But it seemed useful to introduce them with a few essays of a different kind in Part I of the book. In three of these, "The Claim of the Living", "Caution and Criticism" and "In a Library", the reader will find the first expression of the author's ideas about reviewing and criticism. Since these essays belong roughly to the period when the majority of the others included here were written, they contribute to an understanding of their general spirit and help to place them in perspective. "Winged Phrases", which discusses George Moore's critical achievement, could have been placed in the first part of the selection; yet its more general interest induced me to put it in Part II next to the essay on *Esther Waters*. "Women Novelists" deals with one of Virginia Woolf's favourite themes: I felt I could not omit this early stage in a life-long trend of thought and writing. And finally, Samuel Butler looms too large in Virginia Woolf's background to be omitted. His chronological position, half-way between past and present, may account for his absence from the previous books of essays. His general importance, as well as the admiration and sympathy Virginia Woolf felt for his books and personality, are enough to justify an otherwise questionable inclusion of two articles about him.

In the second part the essays are printed in their order of composition, but, whenever there were reviews of several books by the same author, they have been printed consecutively in chronological order. None of the essays included in this volume has previously been reprinted in a volume of collected essays by Virginia Woolf.

Very many of Virginia Woolf's most important critical essays were published in book form long ago. With *The Captain's Death Bed* (1950), which included among other important essays the pivotal "Mr Bennett and Mrs Brown", it seemed that everything the author of *The Common Reader* thought about literature was available to the public. The publication, two and a half years later (1953), of *A Writer's Diary*, covering an immense field of criticism and throwing a new light on Virginia Woolf's work and personality, confirmed the impression that we had, if not all the desirable material, at least the essential to draw "the figure in the carpet". Of course, one still regretted that the diary was only a writer's diary; one felt the absence of letters; *Virginia Woolf and Lytton Strachey: Letters*, published in 1956, only whetted one's appetite for more; but this is not the place to discuss letters and diaries. Then, to the few who read that sort of book, B. J. Kirkpatrick's *A Bibliography of Virginia Woolf* (1957) revealed that more than one half of Virginia Woolf's essays were still buried in periodicals. *Granite and Rainbow* (1958) was the first step taken by Mr Leonard Woolf to bring to light this hidden treasure. The selection is particularly interesting: it clearly suggests in outline the book Virginia Woolf had long been dreaming of writing: "The Art of Fiction". The second section, entitled "The Art of Biography", although apparently a mere addition to the many portraits hanging on the walls of "Virginia's room" as we knew it, completes the gallery with early essays that take us back to the beginnings of the author's career. Besides, "The New Biography" (1927), which opens this section, shows us the first stages in the forming of her views, which reached their final phase in "The Art of Biography" (1939) included in *The Death of the Moth*.

The essays published in *Granite and Rainbow* have the same themes which underlay and bound together the majority of the essays in the previous collections and therefore admirably supplement them. They do not open new vistas in the literary land travelled by Virginia Woolf: with them we follow the same highways and by-roads of the "great tradition". Apart from a name here, a sentence there, they deal essentially with literature in general or with the authors of the past. They belong to a definite category, criticism, and this justifies the restricted choice of the editor. Even "An Essay in Criticism", which bears on Hemingway's fiction, deliberately and characteristically enough tries to avoid trespassing on the unsafe territory of the neighbouring genre, reviewing. What is adumbrated in this essay of 1927 and later set forth in bolder outline in "Reviewing" (1939) gives the clue to the principles of discrimination which governed Virginia Woolf in her composition of *The Common Reader*, and possibly in the preserving of the essays which she considered of some lasting interest. In editing *Granite and Rainbow*, Mr Leonard Woolf remained faithful to the critic's ideal. However, if we look closer into the full-fledged theory developed in "Reviewing", we discover under all the gusto and imaginative exaggeration of the pamphlet that the shortcomings of this minor form of criticism are not necessarily part and parcel of the genre, if only it were properly understood and practised. Limited to its functions of informing the public and of advertisement, reviewing is both ineffectual and open to criticism, asserts Virginia Woolf. But then, following Harold Nicolson's lead, she suggests that the reviewer should satisfy the desire of authors to be told why he likes or dislikes their works, and he should thus turn himself into an advisor or "consultant, expositor or expounder", as she calls this new doctor for the relief of literary pain. Setting aside the possible weaknesses of the argument and conclusions, which were pointed out by Mr Leonard Woolf in a note appended to the pamphlet, let us consider only the relationship between reviewer and author and the qualities required in the former. He is referred to as "a live human being", "a well-stored mind, knowing other books and even other literatures and thus other standards". Who else, then, can he be but the expert in literature contributing his full personality as well as his knowledge to the analysis and discussion of the book to be examined? He is of course the ideal critic; more precisely still, the casual reference to the "honest and intelligent reader" irresistibly suggests a close kinship between this new type of reviewer and the author of *The Common Reader*. Even though "Reviewing" was written at a time when Virginia Woolf had all but given up reviewing, it is so much in line with all that she wrote about the art of criticism that we can assume that her essays on contemporary literature are worth studying, as they show the same qualities, the same attitudes and preoccupations, as her discussions of the works of the past.

For instance, in her objections to Rowland Thirlmere's and W. Somerset Maugham's way of writing about their travels, we discover an early expression of that sympathy with Sterne of which she was to give many tokens later. She tells of her delight in *A Sentimental Journey*, but at the same time she reveals her distrust of sentiment; often in her diary she seems to be exorcising her fear of falling a victim to it: in this essay she points out the weakness in others while she asserts her classical taste which requires a perfect amalgamation and balance of fact and sentiment, an ideal she strove for in novel after novel.

We knew that she did not like the Edwardian trinity: Bennett, Galsworthy and Wells; we find it gratifying to read in her reviews of their books the specific grounds of her objections: they add weight to the more general criticism with which we are already familiar. Naturally she takes Mr Bennett to task for his realism and his excessive and professional praise of the well-made novel. Yet, she is ready to forgive him simply because he speaks of books as a man who, from personal experience, "knows all that there is to know about the making of books". Is not this knowledge the prerequisite of all good criticism on which she never fails to insist? And here is another example of the various ways in which these essays keep the reader's mind on the alert. We do not know the exact moment when Virginia Woolf first thought of writing "Kew Gardens"; so, when in "Books and Persons" (July 5, 1917) she answers Mr Bennett's question as to the possibility that some writers might do in words what the Neo-Impressionists have done in paint, her challenge sounds like the emergence of the idea out of which the famous sketch was to grow.

In L. P. Jacks's fiction, although her distrust of an excess of intelligence and undue stress on ideas causes her to qualify her praise, she is highly appreciative of the originality of the philosopher's handling of fiction, of his efforts to break new ground; she hails him as an explorer. He may not have "devised a shape" that fits the uncommon booty he brings back from the uncharted regions, the abysses of time and consciousness into which he has wandered, yet, throughout the essay, we feel how deeply roused Virginia Woolf must have been. Her reference to the "shudder of a conservative mind" in front of L. P. Jacks's books is purely rhetorical; there is hardly a sentence which does not express her interest in this fellow revolutionary. Her very detection of his shortcomings shows how carefully and thoughtfully she considered the venture.

Still more interesting in this respect are the two reviews of Dorothy Richardson's novels. No longer kept at a distance by philosophy, theology and a male indulgence in ideas, Virginia Woolf feels more at ease. She could have said, as she put it in her diary about the time she wrote the first review, commenting on a visit to J. Middleton Murry and Katherine Mansfield: "I find it much easier to talk to Katherine." She certainly finds it much easier to talk to Dorothy—since, after all, reviewing is a conversation between reviewer and author. Besides, she was through, then, with the conventional novel, or close enough to the end of *Night and Day* (finished in March 1919), and most probably was looking ahead in the direction she had already explored with "The Mark on the Wall" and had just taken again with "Kew Gardens". What was merely suggested in "Philosophy in Fiction" —as, probably, it had not yet hardened into consistent thinking in the critic's mind—suddenly becomes articulate, sharp and vivid in "The Tunnel". Virginia Woolf finds fault with Dorothy Richardson's achievement, in the same way as she did with L. P. Jacks's. Nevertheless she praises her for her method and her courage in discarding the "old deliberate business", as she irreverently calls the traditional rules of novel writing. The article reads like a rough sketch of "Modern Novels" (reprinted as "Modern Fiction" in *The Common Reader I*) published two months later. Many critics—generally scholarly critics, who never wrote anything but what they have gleaned right and left and more or less skilfully pieced together—many critics have ascribed various sources to Virginia Woolf's novel technique. They certainly will pounce on the new "evidence" produced here, and will claim that it makes it quite clear that Virginia Woolf's new novel is a mere exploitation of Dorothy Richardson's. Far from bearing out this view, I believe on the contrary that the parallelism which exists between the review of "The Tunnel" and "Modern Fiction" shows that Virginia Woolf is no more indebted to Dorothy Richardson than to Arnold Bennett. What is seminal in her reading and analysis of other works is not what is closest or most akin to her own views—that does not enrich her or, at best, it only stimulates her—but precisely what dissatisfies her, what she considers their failings. Neither *Portrait of the Artist as a Young Man*, nor any volume of *Pointed Roofs* can ever give the clue to the originality of *Jacob's Room*. The only thing we can safely say is that Virginia Woolf wanted to write— and she did write—a chronicle that was altogether different from these recent prototypes.

Little more need be said about the present selection. With a few exceptions all the writers discussed here are mentioned either in *A Writer's Diary* or in the essays already gathered in book form; but this new collection offers new visions of them. The reader will welcome a few new topics such as Freudianism—and new angles from which the old ones are viewed. However, the main interest of these pages is that they afford the opportunity, denied us hitherto, to look over Virginia Woolf's shoulder while, pen in hand, according to her habit, she reads her contemporaries. Although she said once: "No creative writer can swallow another contemporary", we can once more appreciate in her this "catholicity of taste" for which David Daiches praised her, and the fairness of judgment which goes along with it. Besides, these essays are illuminating marginalia to her literary theories; they particularly show how she steered her own way between the roads travelled by the writers of her time. While she talks about new books, we see her thinking of her own writing, checking her fellow artists' experiments with her own, eager to praise what corroborates her findings or her aspirations, sensitive to the very faults she most wants to avoid herself. Here, as ever, she appears not in search of novelty for novelty's sake: novelty she recognizes and praises according to its merits; but what she looks for and commends are the sterling values of intelligence, invention, sincerity and personality, which make all real works of art essentially and lastingly new.

October 1964   JEAN GUIGUET

NOTE

With the exception of "Romance and the Heart" (page 123), which appeared in *The Nation & Athenaeum*, all the essays in this book appeared as reviews in the *Times Literary Supplement*.

PART I

The Claim of the Living

Review of *A Novelist on Novels*, by W. L. George.
(13 June, 1918.)

MR GEORGE is one of those writers for whom we could wish, in all kindness of heart, some slight accident to the fingers of the right hand, some twinge or ache warning him that it is time to stop, some check making brevity more desirable than expansion. He has ideas and enthusiasms, prejudices and principles in abundance, but in his fluency he repeats himself, bolsters up good arguments with poor illustrations, and altogether uses more paper than the country can well afford. The following sentence shows how his ideas tend to overlap each other owing to the speed at which they are composed: "Autobiography has had its way with him [Mr E. M. Forster] a little in *A Room with a View*, and very much more in that tale of school-masters *The Longest Journey*, but it was *Howards End*, that much criticized work, which achieved the distinction of being popular, though of high merit." Thus hooking one statement to another Mr George rambles over a great many ideas connected with novelists and their art, and abuses the public at great length for its insolent neglect of the artist. Proof is added to proof. When Lord Curzon, the Bishop of London, and Mr Conrad come into a room which of them causes "a swirl in 'the gilded throng' "? "The attitude of the State to the novelist defines itself most clearly when a royal commission is appointed." What novelist has ever been asked to sit upon a royal commission? What novelist has ever been welcomed as a son-in-law? To cut the matter short, if the present Lord Nelson owns 7,000 acres of land, what is the amount of the pension enjoyed by Leigh Hunt's daughter?

But Mr George's chief claim to attention lies not in this voluble and elementary satire but in the courage with which he has faced his contemporaries. It is a courage that overshoots its mark, but still it needs considerable courage to declare that one has found "more that is honest and hopeful in a single page of Tono-Bungay than in all the great Victorians put together". It needs, oddly enough, some quality rarer than courage and more desirable to have read all the novels mentioned in this book and to hold a serious opinion as to their merits. For it is extremely difficult to take the writings of one's contemporaries seriously. The spirit in which they are read is a strange compact of indifference and curiosity. On the one hand the assumption is that they are certainly bad, on the other the temptation assails us to find in them a queer and illicit fascination. Between these two extremes we vacillate, and the attention we grant them is at once furtive, intermittent and intense. In proof of this let anyone read over the list of seven young novelists accepted by Mr George as the most promising of their generation— Mr Beresford, Mr Cannan, Mr Forster, Mr Lawrence, Mr Compton Mackenzie, Mr Onions and Mr Swinnerton. The list is fairly representative, but certainly if our income depended upon passing an examination in their works we should be sweeping the streets tomorrow. We feel sure that such a test would produce a large army of street sweepers. It is not that we have neglected to order a certain number of their novels from the library. It is not that, on seeing them before us, we have neglected to read them. But our knowledge is perfectly haphazard and nebulous. To discuss the point of view, the growth, nature and development of any one of these writers in the same spirit that we discuss the dead proves impossible. The difficulty which lies at the root of this attitude affects Mr George too, in spite of his enthusiasm for modern fiction and his proud claim for the prose form. He does not find it at all easy to make out what is happening.

The literary tradition is changing and a new one is being made. Perhaps we may divide these seven writers into three groups—self-exploiters, mirror-bearers and commentators.... They stand midway between the expression of life and the expression of themselves. ... A new passion is born, and it is a complex of the old passions; the novelist ... needs to be more positive, to aspire to know what we are doing with the working class, with the Empire, the woman question, and the proper use of lentils. It is this aspiration towards truth that breaks up the old form: you cannot tell a story in a straightforward manner when you do but glimpse it through the veil of the future.

Fiction is becoming chaotic and formless and omnivorous. But the attempt at a general survey, or at any grouping of tendencies, is very vague; and Mr George turns not without relief to the criticism of the novels in detail, to biographical sketches, and even to memories of garden parties on Campden Hill. The criticism is not bad criticism, but it has too great an air of the personal and provisional to be accepted with conviction. There is no perspective, no security about it.

But the fault hardly lies with Mr George and scarcely at all with the novelists. They must live before they achieve the repose which is so much more ornamental than life. They must appear at garden parties and achieve, or fail to achieve, the "swirl" which Mr George thinks a proper tribute to their powers. But they must be content to forgo authoritative criticism until they are long past the age at which they can profit by it. They must put up with the random patronage of people who subscribe to libraries and to the snapshots of reviewers. Meanwhile they enjoy a kind of homage which is not altogether to be despised. We should judge it an immense calamity if all the writers whom Mr George speaks of were destroyed in a single night. Yes, in our condescending, indolent way we are proud of them; we need them; we have a dim consciousness of a band of light upon the horizon which is due to their incessant imaginative fervour, and sometimes we seem to see that from all this agitation and confusion something of great importance is taking shape.

Caution and Criticism

Review of *Modern English Writers*, by Harold Williams.
(3 October, 1918.)

ONE is inclined to say that if Mr Williams had been less
impartial and less conscientious he would have written
a better, at least a more readable, book. If, like most histo-
rians of modern literature, he had written to prove a theory
or impose a view of art, the 360-odd writers whose works he
examines in these pages would have merged themselves
magically in an orderly pattern, which, whether fallacious
or not, we should have taken in at a glance. As it is each
of these writers stands obstinately a little apart from his
fellow; and when Mr Williams, drawing back and half
closing his eyes, tries to resolve them into schools or tendencies he is forced to confess, being an honest man, that he can
see nothing but individuals. That he set out in the hope of
reducing them to some kind of order is obvious from the
opening pages of his book. The year 1890, he does his best to
insist, was the year in which the Victorianism of the Victorian age virtually, or practically, or to some extent, passed
away; but as it was not of one texture, nor disappeared all at
once, owing to the longevity of George Meredith and other
causes, nothing so dramatic as a fresh age could immedi-
ately succeed it. It was replaced gradually by a patchwork
of influences—the significance of Oscar Wilde's aesthetic-
ism, the aims of the Yellow book, and the Savoy; the
influence of W. E. Henley; and the ideals of the Celtic
revival in Ireland. Under these banners we have with
qualifications and exceptions, and, of course, with innumerable inter-alliances and reactions, fought until that other
convenient date—August 1914.

This general statement being very guardedly and ten-
tatively laid down, Mr Williams proceeds to examine into
the cases of particular writers and finds before very long
that it is impossible to keep them even within these sufficiently elastic boundaries. As early as page 68 he finds it
necessary to content himself with the study of separate
writers whose aims become increasingly individual and

disconnected. Then a rough chronological order is attempted, and at one point it seems as if the novelists were to be grouped, not according to their age, but according to their worthlessness. It becomes, indeed, more and more evident, as Mr Williams says, that "we are reading with our eyes too close to the book to see the print distinctly". Hampered by this drawback, and having no ulterior reward to offer himself in the shape of an aesthetic theory, Mr Williams is indefatigable and undaunted. His zeal is comparable to the zeal of the scientist who examines innumerable specimens and yet allows himself to draw no conclusions. The examination, too, seems to be equally thorough, whether the specimen is as rare and curious as Mr Conrad, or as commonplace and abundant as writers whom we refrain from mentioning. His singular lack or disregard of personal preferences leads him to pronounce carefully balanced judgments upon books which, so far as we can see, no more deserve description than the dandelions of the year before last.

A forgotten writer called Henry Dawson Lowry was once apparently compared by his admirers to Keats and Heine. Mr Williams in his careful way finds space to assure us that he has nothing "of Heine's wayward strength, nothing of Keats's wealth of language and picturesque decorativeness," as if we were still in danger of wrecking ourselves upon that obsolete rock. Books whose writers alone can have any interest in their fate are carefully compared, their plots often analysed, and their final worth summed up in phrases which, if they censure, are generally moderately encouraging at the same time. "Mr O'Sullivan has no affectation of startling originality, but he is rarely wholly commonplace." "Auguries (1913) contains grave and regular verse embodying the not too eager musings and emotions of a cultivated thoughtful, but not original, mind." "Her verse is never enhanced by those sudden and illuminating felicities of phrase and thought which mark greater poetry . . . but, on the other hand, she is not frequently disconcertingly empty of matter, and her sentiment rarely degenerates to insipidity." Such things have no doubt to be said in the world we live in, but we have always been sanguine enough to hope that the succeeding week strewed oblivion upon them.

But, making allowance for a certain formal remoteness of manner, which is, no doubt, inevitable considering the numbers to be surveyed, Mr Williams's judgment is uniformly fair and his mind singularly open. He finds a good word not only for Mr Bennett and Mr Wells, but for Mr Tirebuck and Miss Milligan. Most writers, again, set upon a task of such labour would by some means have deluded themselves into the belief that a good number of their vast flock of geese were swans. But Mr Williams is singularly without illusions. He reminds us that "at the beginning of the twenty-first century, in all probability, the great number of the poets named in this book, with all their poems, will only be matter for comparative study by the literary expert".

As to the novelists. "Of those who find a place here the greater number will be forgotten in a few decades." In a mood of intelligible pessimism he tells us indeed that it is better "to read contemporary verse for the joy and inspiration it may afford us individually, untroubled by any desire to speak or write of it". Nevertheless, Mr Williams has been troubled to write, and to some purpose, for though the lack of complete bibliographies and the insufficiency of the biographies will not suit students who seek exact information, a foreigner wishing to take a bird's-eye view of modern English literature will find Mr Williams a safe guide.

In a Library

Review of *A Quiet Corner in a Library*, by William Henry
Hudson. (23 November, 1916.)

WE hope that the modesty of Professor Hudson's preface
will not mislead many of his readers into thinking that
it is quite a simple matter to write such a book themselves. It
is, he says, a by-product of "more serious work in literature",
and unless we are much mistaken, behind each of the essays
lies a background of extremely wide and serious reading.
The learning is suppressed rather than obtruded; but it
raises Professor Hudson to an eminence from which he can
see his subject in the right proportions, and makes his
treatment at once light and authoritative.

Anyone who chances to read an essay now and again
upon such forgotten writers as Henry Carey and George
Lillo is aware how earnestly the essayist strains to prove the
importance of his subject. Either he was the unacknowledged father of the novel or the forgotten originator of the
essay—a claim we would willingly concede, for the most
part, if by so doing we might escape the proofs of it. Professor Hudson, on the other hand, frankly acknowledges the
obscurity of his heroes, and, by demonstrating that their
writing was often extremely dull, persuades us to find a
good deal of amusement in it. But, having all the facts at
his fingers' ends, he can do what is more to the point—he
can show us why it is that men like Carey and Lillo, while
themselves unimportant, are yet interesting figures in the
history of literature.

Carey, we all know, wrote "Sally in our Alley". But we
do not know that he wrote it after "dodging" a shoemaker's
'prentice who was taking his sweetheart to a "sight of
Bedlam, the Puppet-Shows, the Flying Chairs, and all the
elegancies of Moorfields". We do not perhaps know that he
was one of the first writers in that aristocratic age to see the
"beauty of a chaste and disinterested passion, even in the
lowest class of human life". Before his time, chaste and disinterested passions were considered to be the monopoly of
the peerage. It was only when you wrote a comedy or wan-

ted to provide some comic relief that you could introduce the lower classes with propriety. This interesting theory is discussed at greater length in the paper upon George Lillo, whose play, *The London Merchant*, did much to bring middle-class men and women upon the stage not as butts, but as heroes and heroines—a piece of presumption which much offended "the Town", although the play has been acted from 1731 down to our own time, when Sir Henry Irving used to play it in the provinces. As a stout democrat Professor Hudson asserts that the prejudice which made an aristocratic hero essential is nowadays "in the last degree unintelligible". But is that so? Considering the rarity of coronets, the number of lords and ladies in modern fiction is really notable, and must be supported by some demand on the part of the public. And the tendency is not quite so unintelligible or so vicious as Professor Hudson would have it. Without saying that certain kinds of emotion are actually made more dignified by the fact that they are felt by a King or a Queen it is far easier to make them seem dignified. The associations are on the side of the peerage. And who shall say that a line like

Queens have died young and fair

would have the same charm if it were merely girls, or maids, who had died young and fair?

The question, however, is not one of title or no title so much as the more interesting question of realism or romance. It is in this respect that Lillo was a great innovator. His heroes and heroines were not only merchants and clerks, but they felt like merchants and clerks. Their virtues were decency, honesty and thrift; and, however tragic they might be, they spoke in prose. And so, as Professor Hudson observes, we descend to the plays of Ibsen and the modern development of prose fiction. But have we made things any easier for the novelist or the dramatist by widening their scope? Naturally not; for where everything may be written about, the difficulty is to know what to leave out. Our modern problem is that we want to preserve the beauty and romance of the heroic together with what is called character-drawing and likeness to life; and the peerage, if it tempts,

tempts because it puts our characters a little further from us and invests them with a softer light. The whole subject of the middle-class drama and the growth of realism is a very interesting one, and we are glad to see that Professor Hudson proposes to treat it at length in a forthcoming book.

Women Novelists

Review of *The Women Novelists*, by R. Brimley Johnson.
(17 October, 1918.)

BY rights, or, more modestly, according to a theory of
ours, Mr Brimley Johnson should have written a book
amply calculated, according to the sex of the reader, to
cause gratification or annoyance, but of no value from a
critical point of view. Experience seems to prove that to
criticize the work of a sex as a sex is merely to state with
almost invariable acrimony prejudices derived from the
fact that you are either a man or a woman. By some lucky
balance of qualities Mr Brimley Johnson has delivered his
opinion of women novelists without this fatal bias, so that,
besides saying some very interesting things about literature,
he says also many that are even more interesting about the
peculiar qualities of the literature that is written by women.

Given this unusual absence of partisanship, the interest
and also the complexity of the subject can scarcely be over-
stated. Mr Johnson, who has read more novels by women
than most of us have heard of, is very cautious—more apt to
suggest than to define, and much disposed to qualify his
conclusions. Thus, though his book is not a mere study of
the women novelists, but an attempt to prove that they
have followed a certain course of development, we should
be puzzled to state what his theory amounts to. The question is one not merely of literature, but to a large extent of
social history. What, for example, was the origin of the
extraordinary outburst in the eighteenth century of novel
writing by women? Why did it begin then, and not in the
time of the Elizabethan renaissance? Was the motive which
finally determined them to write a desire to correct the
current view of their sex expressed in so many volumes and
for so many ages by male writers? If so, their art is at once
possessed of an element which should be absent from the
work of all previous writers. It is clear enough, however,
that the work of Miss Burney, the mother of English fiction,
was not inspired by any single wish to redress a grievance:
the richness of the human scene as Dr Burney's daughter

had the chance of observing it provided a sufficient stimulus; but however strong the impulse to write had become, it had at the outset to meet opposition not only of circumstance but of opinion. Her first manuscripts were burnt by her stepmother's orders, and needlework was inflicted as a penance, much as, a few years later, Jane Austen would slip her writing beneath a book if anyone came in, and Charlotte Brontë stopped in the middle of her work to pare the potatoes. But the domestic problem, being overcome or compromised with, there remained the moral one. Miss Burney had showed that it was "possible for a woman to write novels and be respectable", but the burden of proof still rested anew upon each authoress. Even so late as the mid-Victorian days George Eliot was accused of "coarseness and immorality" in her attempt "to familiarize the minds of our young women in the middle and higher ranks with matters on which their fathers and brothers would never venture to speak in their presence".

The effect of these repressions is still clearly to be traced in women's work, and the effect is wholly to the bad. The problem of art is sufficiently difficult in itself without having to respect the ignorance of young women's minds or to consider whether the public will think that the standard of moral purity displayed in your work is such as they have a right to expect from your sex. The attempt to conciliate, or more naturally to outrage, public opinion is equally a waste of energy and a sin against art. It may have been not only with a view to obtaining impartial criticism that George Eliot and Miss Brontë adopted male pseudonyms, but in order to free their own consciousness as they wrote from the tyranny of what was expected from their sex. No more than men, however, could they free themselves from a more fundamental tyranny—the tyranny of sex itself. The effort to free themselves, or rather to enjoy what appears, perhaps erroneously, to be the comparative freedom of the male sex from that tyranny, is another influence which has told disastrously upon the writing of women. When Mr Brimley Johnson says that "imitation has not been, fortunately, the besetting sin of women novelists", he has in mind no doubt the work of the exceptional women who imitated neither a sex nor any individual of either sex. But to take no more thought of their sex when they wrote than of the colour of their eyes was one of their conspicuous distinctions, and of itself a proof that they wrote at the bidding of a profound and imperious instinct. The women who wished to be taken for men in what they wrote were certainly common enough; and if they have given place to the women who wish to be taken for women the change is hardly for the better, since any emphasis, either of pride or of shame, laid consciously upon the sex of a writer is not only irritating but superfluous. As Mr Brimley Johnson again and again remarks, a woman's writing is always feminine; it cannot help being feminine; at its best it is most feminine: the only difficulty lies in defining what we mean by feminine. He shows his wisdom not only by advancing a great many suggestions, but also by accepting the fact, upsetting though it is, that women are apt to differ. Still, here are a few attempts: "Women are born preachers and always work for an ideal." "Woman is the moral realist, and her realism is not inspired by any idle ideal of art, but of sympathy with life." For all her learning, "George Eliot's outlook remains thoroughly emotional and feminine". Women are humorous and satirical rather than imaginative. They have a greater sense of emotional purity than men, but a less alert sense of honour.

No two people will accept without wishing to add to and qualify these attempts at a definition, and yet no one will admit that he can possibly mistake a novel written by a man for a novel written by a woman. There is the obvious and enormous difference of experience in the first place; but the essential difference lies in the fact not that men describe battles and women the birth of children, but that each sex describes itself. The first words in which either a man or a woman is described are generally enough to determine the sex of the writer; but though the absurdity of a woman's hero or of a man's heroine is universally recognized, the sexes show themselves extremely quick at detecting each other's faults. No one can deny the authenticity of a Becky Sharp or of a Mr Woodhouse. No doubt the desire and the capacity to criticize the other sex had its share in deciding women to write novels, for indeed that particular vein of comedy has been but slightly worked, and promises great richness. Then again, though men are the best judges of men and women of women, there is a side of each sex which is known only to the other, nor does this refer solely to the relationship of love. And finally (as regards this review at least) there rises for consideration the very difficult question of the difference between the man's and the woman's view of what constitutes the importance of any subject. From this spring not only marked differences of plot and incident, but infinite differences in selection, method and style.

A Man with a View

Review of *Samuel Butler: Author of Erewhon, the Man and his Work*, by John F. Harris. (20 July, 1916.)

IT is probable that any one who reads Samuel Butler will wish to know more about him. He is one of those rare spirits among the dead whom we like, or it may be dislike, as we do the living, so strong is their individuality and so clearly can we make up our minds about their manners and opinions. Johnson is of this company, and we can each add others according to our private tastes; but the number of people who will put Samuel Butler upon their list must be increasing every day. For this reason we would give a good deal to have a life of Butler, with plenty of letters and anecdotes and reports of those private sayings and doings in which surely he must have excelled. Mr Harris has had access apparently to no more information than is already before the public, so that he cannot gratify us in this respect; and at first there may seem little reason for another study of Butler's works when Mr Cannan's book is scarcely a year old. But Mr Harris is quite strong enough to dispel our doubts. He writes clearly and with considerable force; he generates in us a desire to contradict him flatly, and again he makes us sigh, half with relief and half with annoyance, when he says something so true that we have always been on the point of saying it ourselves. His work has the merit, in particular the very clear chapter on the scientific books, of bringing out the main lines of thought which unite all Butler's work, so that instead of thinking him an eccentric who took up subjects much at random, we have a more serious picture of a man who built up solidly a house with many storeys. But the justification of Mr Harris's volume is that directly we have finished it we take down Butler to see what the change in our conception of him amounts to.

All this writing and disputing on his account is, of course, much what Butler himself expected of an intelligent posterity. But why is it that his lamp not only still shines among the living, but with a light that positively grows brighter and seems altogether more friendly and more kindling as

the years go by? Perhaps it is that the other lights are going
out. Certainly Mr Harris paints a very depressing picture
of the great Victorians. There was George Eliot with her
philosophic tea parties; and Tennyson declaiming pom-
pously before the statues in the British Museum; and Pater
with a style that Butler likened to the face of an enamelled
old woman; and Arnold's "odour which was as the faint
sickliness of hawthorn". It was an age, according to Mr
Harris, "of false values and misplaced enthusiasms, unaccountable prejudices, astonishing deficiency in artistic perception, and yet with it a bewildering lack of real practical
efficiency". Whether this is true or not, it represents very
fairly Butler's own point of view. Further on, however, Mr
Harris points out more suggestively that Butler was singular
in being the spectator of his age, an amateur, "a non-
professional worker ... as well as a lover". These words seem
to us to indicate the most vital distinction that there was
between Butler and his contemporaries. The Victorian
age, to hazard another generalization, was the age of the
professional man. The biographies of the time have a
depressing similarity; very much overworked, very serious,
very joyless, the eminent men appear to us to be, and
already strangely formal and remote from us in their likes
and dislikes. Butler, of course, hated nothing more than the
professional spirit; and this may account for the startling
freshness of his books, as if they had been laid up all these
years in sweet-scented roots and pungent spices. Naturally
his fellow-men owed him a grudge (though we should like
more evidence of what Mr Harris calls "the conspiracy"
against him), as schoolboys set to do their sums in a dreary
schoolroom have a grudge against a boy who passes the
window with a butterfly net in his hand and nothing to do
but enjoy himself.

But why, if they were imprisoned, was Butler free? Had
the achievement been an easy one, we should not owe him
the enormous debt of thanks which is his due. To free himself from the fetters which he found so galling it was not
enough by a long way merely to refuse to be a clergyman.
He had to preserve that kind of honesty, originality, or
sensibility which asserts itself whether you are about to

baptize a child or to go to an evening party, and asks, "Now why am I doing this? Is it because other people do it? Is it right? Do I enjoy doing it?" and is always preventing its possessor from falling into step with the throng. In Butler's day, at any rate, such a disposition was fatal to success. He failed in everything he took up—music and science, painting and literature; and lived the most secluded of lives, without need of dress clothes, in a set of rooms in Clifford's Inn, where he cooked his own breakfast and fetched his own water. But his triumph lay not in being a failure, but in achieving the kind of success he thought worth while, in being the master of his life, and in selecting the right things to do with it. Never, we imagine, did Butler have to plead that he was too busy for some pleasant thing, such as a concert or a play, or a visit to a friend. Every summer found him with sufficient pocket money to afford a trip to Italy; his week-end jaunts to the country were conducted with extreme regularity, and we should guess that he seldom put himself out to catch a train. But, above all, he had achieved a freedom of soul which he expressed in one book after another. In his obscurity he had wrought out a very clear notion of "the Kingdom of Heaven" and of the qualities needed by those who seek it; of the people who are the "only people worth troubling about", and of the things "which nobody doubts who is worth talking to". He had, of course, a splendid collection of hatreds, just as he worshipped Handel and Shakespeare, Homer and the authoress of the Odyssey, Tabachetti and Bellini, so as to make him rather suspicious of other worshippers. In his isolation and idiosyncrasies he sometimes recalls Edward FitzGerald, but with the great difference that whereas FitzGerald early realized the vanity of fighting the monster, Butler was always busy planting his darts in the flanks of his age, always pugnacious and always full of self-confidence. And against neglect and disapproval he had a private supply of most satisfactory consolations. It was much better fun, he said, to write fearlessly for posterity than to write "like, we will say, George Eliot, and make a lot of money by it". These reflections certainly kept his temper cooler than is usual in the case of a man who has so much to satirize, and also preserved in all its vigour his most uncompromising individuality. But perhaps his greatest fault as a writer springs from this irresponsibility, his determination, that is, to humour his own ideas in season and out of season, whether they serve to clog the story to stagnation, as sometimes happens in *The Way of All Flesh*, or to give it shade and depth. Very occasionally he reminds one of those eccentric and insistent people who persist in bathing daily in the Serpentine, or in wearing a greatcoat all the year round, and proclaim that such is the only road to salvation. But that trifling defect is the one drawback of the solitude to which he was condemned.

His many-sided training in art and music, sheep-farming and literature, by exposing so many different sides of his mind to the light, kept him amazingly fresh to the end of life; but he achieved this freshness quite consciously also by treating life as an art. It was a perpetual experiment which he was for ever watching and manipulating and recording in his note-books; and if today we are less ambitious, less apt to be solemn and sentimental, and display without shame a keener appetite for happiness, we owe this very largely to Butler's example. But in this, too, he differed very much from his contemporaries.

All these qualities and a thousand more—for Butler is a very complex personality, and, like all great writers, finally inscrutable—are to be found in his books. Of these the most remarkable, perhaps, are *The Way of All Flesh*, and *The Note-books*. He had worked upon both for many years, and the novel he would have written yet again had he lived. As it is, it has all the qualities of work done almost as a hobby, from sheer love of it, taken up and laid down at pleasure, and receiving the very impress of the maker's hand. And yet it is easy to understand why it did not arouse enthusiasm when it first appeared—why it yields more upon the third reading than upon the first. It is a book of conviction, which goes its own way, passing the conventional turnings without looking at them. But, after reading it, we hardly care to inspect some of the masterpieces of English fiction; it would be as unkind as to let in the cold light of day upon a dowager in a ball dress. It would be easy to enumer-

ate many important and splendid gifts in which Butler as a
novelist was deficient; but his deficiency serves to lay bare
one gift in which he excelled, and that is his point of view.
To have by nature a point of view, to stick to it, to follow it
where it leads, is the rarest of possessions, and lends value
even to trifles. This gift Butler had in the highest degree; he
gives a turn or a twist to the most ordinary matter, so that
it bores its way to the depths of our minds, there to stay
when more important things have crumbled to dust. If
proof of this is wanted, read his account of buying new-laid
eggs in *The Note-books*, or the story of "The Aunt, the Nieces,
and the Dog", or the anecdote of the old lady and her parrot
in *The Humour of Homer*. These Note-books of Butler's will
certainly beget many other note-books, which will be a
source of profound disappointment to their owners. It
seems so simple a thing to have a note-book and to have
ideas; but what if the ideas refuse to come, or lodge in the
same place instead of ranging from earth to Heaven? We
shall, at any rate, learn to respect Butler more highly. The
truth is that despite his homeliness and his seeming accessi-
bility, no one has ever succeeded in imitating Butler; to do
so one would have to unscrew one's head and put it on
altogether differently. At one time we think it is his humour
that eludes us, that strange, unlaughing, overwhelming gift
which compresses his stories at one grasp into their eternal
shape; at another the peculiar accent and power of his
style; but in the end we cease to dissect, and give ourselves
up to delight in a structure which seems to us so entire and
all of a piece; so typically English, we would like to think,
remembering his force of character, his humanity, and his
great love of beauty.

The Way of All Flesh

Review of *The Way of All Flesh*, by Samuel Butler.
(26 June, 1919.)

"... like most of those who come to think for themselves, he was a slow grower," says Samuel Butler of Ernest, the hero of *The Way of All Flesh*. The book itself has had the same sort of history, and for much the same reason. For seven years after the first publication in 1903, it sold very slowly. It was reprinted, "widely reviewed and highly praised", but still hung fire. Then, in 1910, the flames caught; twice in that year it was reprinted, and the impression before us is the eleventh of the second edition. A wise author might choose that fate rather than one of more immediate splendour. No reading public is going to be rushed into buying an author who thinks for himself; its instinct of self-preservation protects it from that folly; first it must go through all the processes of inspection and suspicion. But the public is fundamentally sagacious. It makes up its mind after seven years or so as to what is good for it, and when it has made up its mind it sticks to it with dogged fidelity. Therefore, one is not surprised to find that in the year 1915 "Butler's writings had a larger total sale than in any previous year since their publication".

Satisfactory as this record is, it is also much in keeping with the character of *The Way of All Flesh*. The book was written very slowly. Butler worked at it intermittently during twelve years. It is thus like a thing that has grown almost imperceptibly, a cactus or a stalactite, becoming a little shapeless, but more and more solid and sturdy year by year. One can imagine that he had grown too fond of it to part with it. Such a work is too uncompromising to make many friends when it first appears. It bears in every part of it the mark of being a home-made hobby rather than the product of high professional skill. All his convictions and prejudices have been found room for; he has never had the public in his mind's eye. So, just as Butler himself would have appeared in a crowd of fashionable people, *The Way of All Flesh* appeared among the season's novels, awkward, opinionated, angular, perverse. Nor, upon re-reading, does it appear that time has softened these qualities, and, to speak the truth, they are not qualities that are admirable in a novel. The note-book which, according to Butler, every one should carry in his waistcoat pocket, has left that secret post of observation and thrust itself forward. Shrewd, didactic passages taken from its pages constantly block the course of the story, or intrude between us and the characters, or insist that Ernest shall deliver them as if they were his own. For this reason Ernest himself remains a sheaf of papers, written all over with the acute and caustic observations of his maker, rather than an independent young man. Such is the penalty that a writer pays for indulging his hobby too far, even though the hobby be, as it was with Butler, the hobby of using his brain. The scene when Ernest attempts the seduction of Miss Maitland is a proof that when Butler's young men and women stepped beyond the circle illuminated by his keen intelligence they found themselves as thin and faltering as the creations of a tenth-rate hack. They must at once be removed to the more congenial atmosphere of the Law Courts. There are certain scenes, it appears, which must be written a great deal too quickly to allow of the deliberate inspection of a note-book, and viewed with a passion impossible to the disillusioned eyes of the elderly. There is a sense, after all, in which it is a limitation to be an amateur; and Butler, it seems to us, failed to be a great novelist because his novel writing was his hobby.

In every other respect his gifts were such as to produce a novel which differs from most professional novels by being more original, more interesting, and more alive. The elderly and disillusioned mind has this advantage—that it cares nothing what people think of it. Further, its weight of experience makes up for its lack of enthusiasm. Endowed with these formidable qualities and a profound originality which wrought them to the sharpest point, Butler sauntered on unconcernedly until he found a position where he could take up his pitch and deliver his verdict upon life at his ease. *The Way of All Flesh*, which is the result, is thus much more than a story. It is an attempt to impart all that Butler thought not only about the Pontifexes, but about religion, the family system, heredity, philanthropy, education, duty, happiness, sex. The character of Christina Pontifex is rich and solid, because all the clergymen's wives whom Butler had ever known were put into her stew. In the same way Dr Skinner has the juice of innumerable headmasters in his veins, and Theobald is compounded of the dust of thousands of middle-class Englishmen. They are representative, but they are, thanks to Butler's vigorous powers of delineation, distinctly themselves. Christina's habit of daydreaming belongs to her individually, and is a stroke of genius—if Butler did not promptly remind us that it is a little silly to talk about strokes of genius. We should not like to say how often in the course of reading *The Way of All Flesh* we found ourselves thus pulled up. Sometimes we had committed the sin of taking things, like genius, on trust. Then, again, we had fancied that some idea or other was of our own breeding. But here, on the next page, was Butler's original version, from which our seed had blown. If you want to come up afresh in thousands of minds and books long after you are dead, no doubt the way to do it is to start thinking for yourself. The novels that have been fertilized by *The Way of All Flesh* must by this time constitute a large library, with well-known names upon their backs.

PART II

Journeys in Spain

Review of *Letters from Catalonia*, by Roland Thirlmere and *The Land of the Blessed Virgin*, by W. S. Maugham. (26 May, 1905.)

BEFORE going on a journey the question of a guide-book naturally suggests itself. Your need is not altogether simple, and, though many profess to supply it, few, when put to the test, are found to succeed. Baedeker settles your hotel and the amount you are expected to tip the waiter; but one suspects Baedeker as an art critic. The asterisk with which he directs you to the best picture and tells you to a superlative how much praise you must be prepared to expend seems too simple a solution of the difficulties of criticism. But though you consult him surreptitiously it is often solely upon him that you come to depend. His work, as generations of grateful travellers can testify, is a necessity, though hardly a luxury. No one thinks of reading him for pleasure, for the reason, perhaps, that his is the most impersonal of books, and even tourists like to be treated as human beings. He provides materials in abundance, but expects you to draw your own conclusions. Thus the traveller when he comes to choose finds that guide-books separate themselves into two classes, and neither gives him completely and compactly what he wants. Books of the type of those that lie before us disclaim, if they do not despise, the name of guide-book. Sterne, when he invented the title of Sentimental Journey, not only christened but called into existence a class of book which seems to grow more popular the more we travel and the more sentimental we become. It is their aim to provide all that Baedeker ignores; but as their aim is more ambitious so is their success very rarely so complete. The Sentimental Journeys that succeed are among the most delightful books in the language; Sterne succeeded and so did Borrow, and Kinglake, and Lord Dufferin, and Mr Henry James. But the list, if we count the competitors, is not a long one. Theirs are books that we may read with almost equal pleasure in the country that they describe or seated a thousand miles away with no prospect of ever seeing the place except with the mind's eye. They owe their success not to any strangeness in the things they saw or to any adventures they met with on the way, but to the faculty of seeing they had in them and of interpreting the sight to others. A book such as this is as much a guide-book to the mind of the man that wrote it as it is to any definite region of the earth's surface. At the same time, the balance is kept even; the sentiment is not allowed to displace the fact, however deeply it colours it. *The Bible in Spain*, for instance, gives a clear portrait both of Borrow and of Spain, but it would be hard to say where Spain ends and Borrow begins. Such an amalgamation demands rare literary genius, and it is no harsh criticism of the writers before us if we say that the secret is not theirs.

Mr Thirlmere gives us two substantial volumes of *Letters from Catalonia*, in which there is considerably more information about Mr Thirlmere than about Catalonia. Catalonia, we gather, is a place which, like many others, possesses sunsets and stars and mosquitoes and cathedrals. Mr Thirlmere has a great deal that is pleasant to say upon all these subjects, and they give rise to reflections which lead us in many directions not marked upon the map of Spain. The sentiment is out of all proportion to the journey. It is but fair to say that we are warned beforehand that many changes will be rung on certain subjects, "such as sunsets, rustic wit, Germany, politics, and so forth"; and when he reaches his 800th page Mr Thirlmere is genuinely surprised to find how seldom he has found it necessary to allude to Catalonia. The book then consists of a miscellaneous collection of meditations and facts and personal opinions which conceal any definite outline of Catalonia as behind a shifting veil. The traveller will still need his Murray; but the two large volumes, though they make no special appeal to travellers, can be read with pleasure by any one who has a taste for light reading of a miscellaneous nature. The value of the book is much increased by the many excellent reproductions of pictures and photographs of Spain, especially of the drawings of Mr Frank Brangwyn.

Mr Somerset Maugham's single volume, *The Land of the Blessed Virgin*, is slim and reticent. He writes of Andalusia, and, so to speak, edits the country carefully. He selects certain scenes which have remained in his mind as typical and illustrative of the country which he knows so well, and they are not necessarily those prescribed by the guide-book. In his work, too, the personal element preponderates; he is content in more than one instance to let an impression stand as a permanent record which was admittedly coloured by facts of purely personal significance. But he has his pen well under control, and strikes out pictures now and again which are true in themselves and yet could have been so seen by one person only. "Ah, the beautiful things which I have seen which other men have not!" he exclaims, and he has a sincere desire to find the right word for the beauty which he genuinely loves and which, consequently, interests him more than any peculiarities in the individual who observes it. His book thus, even when the desire is beyond his power of satisfying it, has a value of its own, both for the traveller and for the reader who remains in his study chair.

The Sentimental Traveller

Review of *The Sentimental Traveller*, by Vernon Lee.
(9 January, 1908.)

IT is, perhaps, the confession of a narrow spirit, but have
we not heard a little too much lately about this pervasive
Genius Loci? Nature has innumerable beauties and defects;
the smallest congregation of cottages is of profound significance; and the more we feel this or see how it can be felt the
more we resent the incessant evocation by one writer after
another of a spirit that we believe to be in its purity both
remote and austere. Vernon Lee, who gives us *The Sentimental Traveller*, in particular boasts the utmost familiarity
with this demon; she looks out of a train window, or parts
her bedroom curtains of a morning, and the picture, compounded partly from the shape of the land, partly from such
expression as human habitation has given it, composes itself
at once. But this is the bodily form only in which the genius
manifests itself; the spirit of the sight travels everywhere,
and wakens echoes in her mind of people, of her childhood,
of music, of books, or perhaps she is led by it to consider
some deep question of life or morality. Her method then, so
far as the portrait of the place is concerned, is purely impressionist, for if she were to concentrate her mind upon the task
of seeing any object as exactly as it can be seen there would
be no time for these egotistical diversions. And who but
pedants and antiquaries want to know when a palace was
built, or the exact style of its architecture? To separate herself emphatically from such worthies she will indulge in quite
gratuitous ambiguities. "To the earlier Greeks, navigating
the dangerous Adriatic, the sun sets visibly among the sea-
girt cones; hence Phaeton, Icarus, and Geryon, who, if you
remember, was in some manner connected with the Hes-
perides. . . ." The dots are a characteristic device, and part
of an artistic system that prevails throughout. If only, in
travelling, you will open your mind to receive all impressions and force your imagination to track down the most
fugitive of suggestions, something charming and valuable,
because original, will be recorded. This is perhaps the

course that any sensitive mind adopts naturally, though it does not always go on to trace it out upon paper. But what art is needed to give such perishable matter an enduring form!—the art of Charles Lamb or of Henry James. Vernon Lee, with much of the curiosity, the candour, and the sensitiveness to trifles of the true essayist, lacks the exquisite taste and penetrating clearness of sight which make some essays concentrated epitomes of precious things. Such phrases as "that bathing-place of dim Napoleonic Grecian-Pilaster and lyre-backed-chair fashionableness" or "the poor, pomatum-locked, faintly mustachioed, wasp-waisted grandson" attempt to snatch the essential; but they surely light on something quite different. Or when the process is reversed, and a waistcoat button is made the centre of branching avenues of thought, do we feel that they strike inevitably from the spot of heat in the middle? "That he [Goethe] should have brought back just this basket seems so human and touching, opening vistas of the kind of memories he, like some others among us, would clutch at; mornings in Verona market-place and such like. Or perhaps" . . . That is slipshod thinking, and if it does stumble on the truth we feel inclined to congratulate ourselves on the accident. The question as to what exactly distinguishes the truth from the falsehood in such work is a delicate one, and the value of the book depends entirely upon our immediate certainty—this is precisely right. We can hardly appeal to any standard but that of our own taste in such matters; why, for instance, does an image like the following satisfy us—"That melancholy sunset, the smell of torn-up seaweed and wet sands, has always remained in my mind as symbolical of a soul's shipwreck"—when the comparison that follows between the shell-fish and the human beings seems altogether forced and unimaginative? "Of such quivering slime we also are made up; and our microscopic realities steep in our living liquids as these creatures in the sea." Perhaps the most satisfactory essays in the book are those that treat of real people, for their characters are more profoundly realized, and are not too fragile to stand a delicate and sure examination.

The Inward Light

Review of *The Inward Light*, by H. Fielding Hall.
(27 February, 1908.)

A N Englishman travelling for business in Burma fell from
his pony and broke his leg. The monks from the monastery above found him and laid him in a dim room, and
bound his head with leaves. He slept and woke in peace, and
looked from his windows over a great valley and heard only
the murmur of cattle, and the cries of peasants, down below,
and at dawn and sunset the melodious chant of Gregorian
prayers. When his own people came to carry him away with
them he begged to be left where he was, telling them of all
the things round him—the fields, the air, the monks, the
children who sang—that refreshed him, and added "I am
quite happy". Indeed, when he was recovered and could
walk out in the country the simplest and most usual sights
delighted and surprised him; not only had they a fresh
beauty of their own, but he became aware that each plant or
animal had in it a soul akin to his soul which made of the
earth one coherent and harmonious whole. To share in this
gave a new meaning to life; "To live was good". And then,
as readers of Mr Fielding Hall's works will expect, the
Englishman of the present volume "began to think". Why
should this accidental stay at a wayside monastery so change
the view of a mature man, who had spent his life in various
travel and effort and had achieved success? Again he resis-
ted the invitation of his friends to return to them, and met
their half scornful questioning with gentle but resolute
replies. He determined that he would set himself to learn
the clearly visible faith which makes the Eastern life so
different from the Western, and decided that the fundamental difference was to be found in the consciousness,
which the Burmese at least still cherish, of the live presence,
the message, of nature. Inspired with this belief he lived on
in the midst of the people and put to them the questions
that no European asks of another. "What is it you think of
life? What is man's soul?" The state of civilization in which
these questions are naked and urgent provides also an

atmosphere of such clarity that very broad answers are possible. In the same spirit, Mr Fielding Hall makes use again and again, with gentle persistency, of the old images; life is a stream, a wind; it is a shaft of sunlight—composed of separate beams, indeed, but you may not part them and bid one burn in the lamp and another in the grate. It is a tide flowing in different measure, but not in different kind, through every living thing, through plants and beasts and man; and they are not units in themselves, but "fractions of [infinity] and must be joined to make One". That is something of what the people told him, and of what was borne in upon him by the sight of their simple ways, and the voice, for such it became, of the beautiful and happy world of nature. He was further told, in answer to his questioning, that the soul of man had been evolved, together with his body, through countless centuries, but the soul has a separate consciousness of its own which is not transmitted to the children of its body, with their physical form. What then happens to it? Is it merged in the wind? No; the monk shook his head. "It goes on for ever, until—until—... Why should we wish to know?" A steamer coming up the river soon afterwards, "a myriad-jewelled water creature breasting the stream", provided the parable of the lamp with the light in it, which is put out, and the energy that made it goes —who knows where? "Tout lasse, tout casse, tout passe. Et tout renaît."

Such fragments of wisdom, though expressed with all Mr Fielding Hall's usual charm of diction, will never perhaps satisfy a mind which asks for counsel earnestly; they are too vague, too slight, too humble. But then, as the author himself would urge, he has never desired to impose the faith of "this little people in their Eastern valley" upon the virile and indomitable West. He is the first to recognize its limitations; but also he is convinced of the value of certain qualities which he finds in the one belief and not in the other. And, as we are all concerned with the business of living, though few consider it philosophically, the impressions of so sensitive an observer have charm and value also. There are, it seems, two distinguishing qualities in the Burmese faith— it makes them happy and it keeps them unafraid. It teaches them that the life of the world from the beginning has been a continuous procession of all its parts towards the infinite light, and that none of the attributes of life are important compared with the capacity for life which is in each; for it is that, the simple living in the midst of other live things, that confers the supreme happiness. Thus they make no distinction between one class and another; their sexes, with different duties, are of equal value; no sharp division of creed or race can separate men who all breathe alike. In order that you may realize the purity of this existence the better, a European who has become a Burman in religion without adopting their conception of the whole passes through one of their merry festivals, and painfully disturbs it; his face is sharp and white and sad. He has come from a land where the faith is dry and formal, as a thing enclosed in sealed vessels; his soul cannot melt into the universal harmony; it is a "little nut within a changing kernel". So, when the famine came it found a meek and acquiescent victim in the race which had no fear of death; "Famines come and go—only the soul lasts on"; and, when the Englishman listened to the prayers of men and women tortured and left desolate, he did not hear bitter words of revolt or hopeless words of submission, but a peaceful sound "like the murmur of the pigeons on the flags". Indeed, the impression which the book leaves, in part perhaps unconsciously, is one of singular peace, but also of singular monotony. The continued metaphors in which their philosophy is expressed, taken from the wind and light, waters, chains of bubbles and other sustained forces, solve all personal energy, all irregularity, into one suave stream. It is wise and harmonious, beautifully simple and innocent, but, if religion is, as Mr Hall defines it, "a way of looking at the world", is this the richest way? Does it require any faith so high as that which believes that it is right to develop your powers to the utmost?

One Immortality

Review of *One Immortality*, by H. Fielding Hall.
(4 February, 1909.)

THERE are a certain number of people who share Mr
William Watson's feeling about the world:

> I have never felt at home,
> Never wholly been at ease—

and are for ever musing upon their discomfort and asking
themselves what it means. Some such discontent seems to
be the natural lot of poets, and, even when it is vague and
fruitless, it is at any rate a step in the right direction—the
first step perhaps towards making something better. Thus
we can imagine an audience to whom Mr Fielding Hall, the
author of *One Immortality* brings consolation, and we must be
careful in dealing with his words to sympathize with the
feeling that prompts them. The need for such a book as this,
indeed, is not obvious, unless one bears these considerations
in mind. It is cast in the form of a novel, but it has nothing in
common with the ordinary novel; it is much taken up with
general questions upon life and conduct, but it is neither
accurate nor profound; and, finally, although one book is
called the West and another the East, there is little of that
gentle and charming account of Eastern beliefs that gave
Mr Hall's previous books their interest. A number of people
travelling to India meet at Venice and become fellow-
voyagers for the rest of the journey. Some are happily
married, and others unhappily; there are nuns on board the
ship, a learned German professor, an Indian girl going
home, a certain Mr Holt, and a girl called Miss Ormond.
But to supply them with names is to put the picture out of
perspective; a name implies substance, passions, and a number of relationships, and Mr Hall's figures have no more
flesh than will cover a single point of view. It is, indeed, a
modern version of the old allegory; the men and women are
brought together solely in order that one may ask a question
and another may answer it. There was never a gentler
prophet than Mr Hall, but still it is as a prophet, gifted with

the sense of what things are not and what things should be, that he comes among us. He feels that the West has forgotten how to live, but it is difficult to say what this means precisely, or how it is to be reformed. The things that he sees and hears suggest to him meditations and explanations. When he sits in the Piazza at Venice, for example, and hears the band play he reflects that "the nation which first learns how to bring back the music to the battle line will sweep the world". He goes on to dwell upon the modern doctrine of efficiency, and the mistake of thinking that human beings are machines; and then his train of thought swells into a mystic rhapsody in which it is said that "all music is a march, a dance, a requiem, or between them. . . . All life is love or war, and ends in death. . . . The sweetest music is the saddest; the least sad is that which drives to war. That is a truth of life". If the company in the Piazza had been in the mood for it, these remarks might have led to a prolonged argument, and Mr Hall would have deserved the thanks of the party for setting up a theory to be pulled in pieces. But as it is, the argument must be carried on in silence, and we are hard put to it to find some term which shall express Mr Hall's form of thought without suggesting that it pretends to be more than it is. The greater part of the book is devoted to a discussion of love; and the different standpoints of men and women, East and West, religious people, and learned men are touched upon, illustrated, and so turned that they seem to make parts of a simple whole. Is not this the secret of Mr Hall's popularity? Phrases like "marriage is the union of man and woman into one organism", or "the souls of all are part of the World Soul that lives for ever" have an Eastern charm about them, as though they were uttered by some placid philosopher, sitting in the road way, in his rags. And there is virtue surely in the position of one who takes nothing for granted, and is always ready to discuss the universe.

A Room with a View

Review of *A Room with a View*, by E. M. Forster.
(22 October, 1908.)

MR E. M. FORSTER'S title *A Room with a View* is symbolical, of course; and to explain the sense which he conveys by it will introduce our comment also. Lucy Honeychurch and her elderly cousin Charlotte go to stay at a pension in Florence; their rooms, they grumble, have no view. A gentleman promptly exclaims, "I have a view; I have a view", and proceeds to offer them his room and the room of his son George. They are outraged, but they consent; and when cousin Charlotte has insisted that she shall occupy the young man's apartment, because he is a bachelor, she discovers, pinned over the washstand, "an enormous note of interrogation". "What does it mean? she thought. . . . Meaningless at first, it gradually became menacing, obnoxious, portentous with evil." But if we are not cousin Charlotte, in age or temper, if, moreover, we have read what Mr Forster has written in the past, we are amused rather than bewildered. We are more than amused, indeed, for we recognize that odd sense of freedom which books give us when they seem to represent the world as we see it. We are on the side, of course, of Mr Emerson and his son George, who say exactly what they mean. We care very much that Lucy should give up trying to feel what other people feel, and we long for the moment when, inspired by Italy and the Emersons, she shall burst out in all the splendour of her own beliefs. To be able to make one thus a partisan is so much of an achievement, the sense that one sees truth from falsehood is so inspiriting, that it would be right to recommend people to read Mr Forster's book on these accounts alone. If we are honest, we must go on to say that we are not so confident by the time the book is at an end. The story runs simply enough. Lucy is kissed by George Emerson, and the ladies fly to Rome. In Rome they meet Mr Cecil Vyse, a young man who feels of his own accord what other people feel, both about art and about life. When Lucy is back again in her ugly home in Surrey she agrees to marry Mr Vyse. But happily the Emersons take the villa over the way, and Lucy is made to own that she can tell the true from the false before it is too late. To compress the motive of the book into this compass is, of course, to simplify it absurdly, for nothing is said of the cleverness, the sheer fun, and the occasional beauty of the surrounding parts. We sketch the story thus, however, because we believe that it was meant to take this line, and we are conscious of some disappointment when for one reason or another it goes a different way, and the view is smaller than we expected. The disappointment is not due to any change of scene, but to some belittlement, which seems to cramp the souls of the actors. Lucy's conversion becomes a thing of trifling moment, and the views of George and his father no longer spring from the original fountain. But should we complain when we have originality and observation, and a book as clever as the other books that Mr Forster has written already?

The Park Wall

Review of *The Park Wall*, by Elinor Mordaunt.
(31 August, 1916.)

*T*HE PARK WALL confirms us in our belief that Elinor Mordaunt takes a very high place among living novelists and also a very honourable one. The book, indeed, is good enough to make us cast our eyes back to the old novels of great reputation, not merely to make the old comparisons and declare that here at last we have a writer worthy, &c., &c.; but to see how far we have travelled and in what respects we differ. Mrs Mordaunt's books appear to us sufficiently original and therefore emphatic to serve as a landmark. She writes in her way, and they in theirs; and one writer may be more richly gifted than another: but that sometimes seems to be of less importance than to have, as only true artists have, a world of one's own; and we begin to think that, whether big or small, Mrs Mordaunt's world is certainly her own.

The Park Wall is a wall of solid bricks, for Alice Ingpen, the heroine, lives in a substantial country house, but it is also a wall of tough though immaterial prejudice. Although she is by nature very slow and diffident, Alice soon finds herself amazingly further outside her park wall than most young women of her station. In the first place, her marriage takes her to live at Terracine, an island which lies "a species of blister on the hot face of the Indian Ocean"; and then her husband turns out to be "a common low cad", a speculator, a gambler, and, naturally, a completely unfaithful husband. By means of a stratagem he sends her back to England on the same ship with a man to whom she has no tie save that of friendship; and directly they land he proceeds to divorce her. Her family shut their park gates against her. A child is born to her, and she goes to live in the South of London, where eventually she finds work in a factory for making cheap dresses. We may add that the story, after many more complications than we have described, ends happily; but the story is not the important thing.

If it were the important thing there would be faults to

find with it—the husband's stratagem, to begin with, is not
a very convincing one; nor can we believe that a respectable
family of country gentlefolk would bring themselves to
desert their daughter, as the Ingpens deserted Alice. But
does it very much matter? So long as the writer moves from
point to point as one who follows the lead of his mind fearlessly, it does not seem to matter at all. Mrs Mordaunt's
mind is an extremely honest one, and where it points, she
follows. She takes us with her, therefore, our intelligence on
the alert, uncertain what is to happen, but with an increasing consciousness that all that happens is part of a genuine
design. The writer is sufficiently mistress of her art to hold
this out firmly before us, without any of those sudden im-
mersions in this character or that incident which overcome
the ill-equipped writer and destroy his composition. Her
mastery of her subject allows her to enrich it with reflections
of real profundity:

> In the romance of young lovers there is the bud; in marriage
> there is the real fruit, sweet or bitter, as the case may be.
> Those who have their teeth in the rind may be slow to discover
> its flavour, for there is a sort of shock of the taste which for a
> while conceals taste. But while they are still uncertain the
> onlookers know all about it; wait, with some interest, for the
> inevitable grimace, and then go away. The man or woman
> who thinks to keep them amused by going on grimacing is
> mistaken.

This ability to withdraw slightly and see the picture as a
whole and reflect upon it is very rare; it generally implies,
as we think it does in the case of Mrs Mordaunt, a power
to strike out characters with solid bodies and clear-cut
features. Her men (unless we are merely hypnotized to
think so by a woman's name on the title page) are less good
than her women; but even they fill their spaces in the design
satisfactorily, and Alice herself is extraordinarily successful.
We feel ourselves thinking so closely with her that, as in the
case of a living person, we almost anticipate her words.
Mrs Mordaunt treats her without any of the self-consciousness and the random boldness which mark her portraits of
men, and makes us wonder whether the most successful

work in fiction is not done almost instinctively. Again, we find ourselves glancing back at the classics. But if anyone seeks proof that the moderns are attempting and achieving something different from the great dead, let him read the scene in the Bloomsbury hotel, when the family spirit utters itself in scarcely articulate cries and curses, with a curious effect as of angry parrots fluttering in a cage round some mute dove with folded wings. Surely Mrs Mordaunt is here attempting something that the Victorians never thought of, feeling and finding expression for an emotion that escaped them entirely. But whether this is so or not, the fact remains that *The Park Wall* is separate and individual enough to be studied for itself.

Before Midnight

Review of *Before Midnight*, by Elinor Mordaunt.
(1 March, 1917.)

BEFORE reviewing Mrs Elinor Mordaunt's new volume of short stories, *Before Midnight*, we ought to confess two, perhaps unreasonable, prejudices: we do not like the war in fiction, and we do not like the supernatural. We can only account for the first of these prejudices by the feeling that the vast events now shaping across the Channel are towering over us too closely and too tremendously to be worked into fiction without a painful jolt in the perspective; but, reasonable or unreasonable, this feeling is roused by one of Mrs Mordaunt's stories only. Better reasons for disliking the use of the supernatural might be given, especially in the case of a writer like Mrs Mordaunt, who has shown in her novels so great a gift for presenting the natural. Nobody can deny that our life is largely at the mercy of dreams and visions which we cannot account for logically; on the contrary, if Mrs Mordaunt had devoted every page of her book to the discovery of some of these uncharted territories of the mind we should have nothing but thanks for her. But we feel a little aggrieved when the writers who are capable of such delicate work resort instead to the methods of the conjurer and ask us to be satisfied with a trick.

As an example of what we mean let us take the second story, "Pan". Here a fashionable lady, who is recovering her health in the north meets a man out fishing who possesses himself of her heart in the most immediate and mysterious way, so that she follows him every day without knowing who he is, and is finally drowned at night in her endeavour to cross the river to reach him. All this is an allegory—but it is founded upon a theory which might form the basis of a deeply interesting study.

Yes, the country is a dangerous place if one once lets oneself become intimate with it, slipping one's soul free from the stolid correctness of country folk, that correctness which has gained them the reputation of piety, and is, really, due to lack

of imagination. For the fact is this: only the stolid, the unimaginative remain; the rest have gone back to the gods.

That seems to promise extremely well. But to drag in the
pointed ears, the shaggy hoofs, the strange music of the
hemlock pipes in exchange for an analysis of the lady's state
of mind seems to us equivalent to saying that the situation is
too difficult to be pursued any further. Mrs Mordaunt has,
as usual, so many shrewd and original things to say about
the men and women of flesh and blood before she has recourse to magic that we resent the powers of darkness more
than ever.

But it is not fair to say that she always avails herself of
these short cuts. The first story in the book is rather a study
in heredity than in magic, and so is the last; and there are
traces in both of them of that individuality which, whether
it is the result of saying what one thinks or whether it is a
special grace of nature, is certainly among the most refresh-
ing of gifts. At the same time we must own that we like Mrs
Mordaunt best when she is most resolutely matter-of-fact.
Indeed, it is when she is keeping strictly to what she has
observed that we catch sight of those curious hidden things
in human life which vanish instinctively directly there is
talk of ghosts or of gods.

South Wind

Review of *South Wind*, by Norman Douglas. (14 June, 1917.)

WE have no quarrel with the shape or size or colour of this novel; but we believe that if, instead of being a brown, plump, freshly printed volume, it were slim, a little yellow, the date about 1818, the cover of a faded green, marked, perhaps, with the rim of an ancient tea cup—if, in short, it resembled the first edition of *Nightmare Abbey* or *Crotchet Castle*—there would be people willing to sift the old bookstalls in search of it, to pay a sovereign for it: people fond of taking it from the shelf and reading their favourite passages aloud, and apt to remark, when they put it back again, "What a pity it is that novelists don't write like this nowadays!" They very seldom do write like this. But when the reader, a few pages deep and beginning to feel settled in the new atmosphere, collects himself, his first comment is likely to be that it is a very strange thing that no one has thought of writing this book before Mr Douglas. The comment is a compliment, although there is a trace of annoyance in it. It signifies that the idea is one of those fresh and fruitful ideas that have been sailing just out of range on the horizon of our minds and now have been brought to shore and all their merchandise unladen by another.

Take all the interesting and eccentric people you can think of, put them on an island in the Mediterranean beyond the realms of humdrum but not in those of fantasy: bid them say shamelessly whatever comes into their heads: let them range over every topic and bring forth whatever fancy, fact, or prejudice happens to occur to them: add, whenever the wish moves you, dissertations upon medieval dukes, Christianity, cookery, education, fountains, Greek art, millionaires, morality, the sexes: enclose the whole in an exquisite atmosphere of pumice rocks and deep blue waves, air with the warm and stimulating breath of the South Wind—the prescription begins something in this way. But we have left out the most important element of all. We are at a loss to define the quality of the author's mind, his way

of presenting these men and women, of turning his ideas.
We glance at Peacock, and then, for a second, at Oscar
Wilde. Peacock is superbly eccentric and opinionated;
Wilde is persuasive and lucid. Mr Douglas possesses these
qualities, but they are his own. His book has a distinguished ancestry, but it was born only the day before yester-
day. So individual is the character of his mind that as we
read we frequently congratulate him upon having found
the right form for a gift that must have been hard to suit. As
frequently we congratulate ourselves on the fact that the
whole affair is turning out so surprisingly and delightfully
successful.

Upon the Island of Nepenthe, then, "an islet of volcanic
stone rising out of the blue Mediterranean", are congre-
gated for various reasons a great many people of marked
idiosyncrasy—Mr Keith, Mr Eames, Miss Wilberforce,
Mr and Mrs Parker, Count Caloveglia, Mme Steynlin, Mr
Denis, and the Duchess of San Martino, to name only the
most prominent. The Bishop of Bampopo, Mr Heard,
alights here for a short stay on his way home from episcopal
duties in the Equatorial Regions. He is introduced to them
all one after another. We scarcely venture to attempt any
summary of their characters or of their conversation. We
may say, however, that Mr Eames was engaged in annota-
ting Perrelli's *Antiquities*. But "it is not true to say that
he fled from England to Nepenthe because he forged his
mother's will, because he was arrested while picking the
pockets of a lady at Tottenham Court-road Station, because he refused to pay for the upkeep of his seven illegiti-
mate children". None of this is true at all. He once had a
love affair, certainly, which left him chronically sensitive on
the subject of balloons. But Mr Eames was the reverse of
Mr Keith. Mr Keith collected information for its own sake.
"He could tell you how many public baths existed in
Geneva in pre-Reformation days, what was the colour of
Mehemet Ali's whiskers, why the manuscript of Virgil's
friend Gallius had not been handed down to posterity, and
in what year and what month the decimal system was introduced into Finland." His was a complex character; he held
marked and peculiar views upon the origin of our English

spleen; he was an epicure; and, "chaster than snow as a conversationalist, he prostituted his mother tongue in letter-writing to the vilest of uses". We are not surprised on the whole that "friends of long standing called him an obscene old man". Of Mrs Parker we need only say that she treasured and displayed in her drawing-room a piece of fine blue material fished from the floating *débris* of a millionaire's yacht, from which she deduced and expressed certain opinions as to the habits of travelling millionaires. Of the millionaire himself, what can be said? The Malthusian philosophy had no more distinguished supporter, and the part he played when in the opinion of the island it became necessary to protect Miss Wilberforce from herself was much to his credit. This poor lady, of unblemished descent and connexions, having lost her lover at sea had taken to the bottle and given way to noctambulous habits, when she was liable to divest herself of her raiment. The Duchess, it is true, was not a duchess at all, but as she talked and behaved like one the right was conceded her. Mme Steynlin, on the other hand, "cared little what frocks she wore so long as somebody loved her". The reader must imagine how they talked, and how one of them was induced incidentally to slip over the edge of a precipice.

But as we have left out all mention of the Alpha and Omega Club of Buddha and the Little White Cows, together with innumerable other interesting and delightful facts, we must cease to summarize. Indeed, a summary of their conduct and conversation is too likely to give the impression that the characters are merely a gallery of whimsical grotesques, mouthpieces for the brilliant and well-informed mind of their author. That is far from the truth. There are an astonishing number of things that never get into novels at all and yet are of the salt of life; and the achievement of *South Wind* is that it has arrested a great number of these things and proved once more what a narrow convention the novelist is wont to impose on us. Meanwhile, although the hot season has dispersed the original party, Mr Keith is still in residence; Mrs Roger Rumbold, the advocate of Infanticide for the Masses, and Mr Bernard, author of the *Courtship of Cockroaches*, have lately arrived. How often in the coming months will our thoughts seek relief if not repose in the Island of Nepenthe, and with what eagerness shall we await a further and even fuller report of its history!

Books and Persons

Review of *Books and Persons*, by Arnold Bennett.
(5 July, 1917.)

THERE are two kinds of criticism—the written and the
spoken. The first, when it gets into print, is said to be
the cause of much suffering to those whom it concerns; but
the second, we are inclined to think, is the only form of
criticism that should make an author wince. This is the
criticism which is expressed when, upon finishing a book,
you toss it into the next armchair with an exclamation of
horror or delight, adding a few phrases by way of comment,
which lack polish and ignore grammar but contain the
criticism which an author should strain all his forces to over-
hear. If criticism can ever help, he will be helped; if it can
ever please, he will be enraptured; the pain, even, is salu-
tary, for it will be severe enough either to kill or to reform.
One or two writers there are who can put this criticism into
prose; but for the most part the adjectives, the grammar,
the logic, the inkpot—to say nothing of humanity and good
manners—all conspire to take the dash and sincerity out of
it, and by the time speech becomes a review there is nothing
left but grammatical English.

Mr Arnold Bennett is one of the few who can catch their
sayings before they are cold and enclose them all alive in
very readable prose. That is why these aged reviews (some
are nearly ten years old) are as vivacious and as much to the
point as they were on the day of their birth. They have
another claim upon our interest. They deal for the most part
with writers who are still living, whose position is still an
open question, about whom we feel more and probably
know more than we can with honesty profess to do about
those dead and acknowledged masters who are commonly
the theme of our serious critics. At the time when Mr Bennett was Jacob Tonson of the *New Age*, Mr Galsworthy,
Mr Montague, Mrs Elinor Glyn, Mr W. H. Hudson, Mr
John Masefield, Mr Conrad, Mr E. M. Forster, Mr Wells
and Mrs Humphry Ward were not exactly in the positions

which they occupy today. The voice of Jacob Tonson had something to do with the mysterious process of settling them where, as we think, they will ultimately dwell. It is true that we are not going to rank any book of Mr Galsworthy's with *Crime and Punishment*, and we dissent a little from the generosity of the praise bestowed upon the novels of Mr Wells. But these are details compared with the far more important question of Mr Bennett's point of view. We have said that his is spoken criticism; but we hasten to add that it is not at all what we are accustomed to hear spoken at dinner-tables and in drawing-rooms. It is the talk of a writer in his workroom, in his shirt-sleeves. It is the talk, as Mr Bennett is proud to insist, of a creative artist. "I am not myself a good theorizer about art," he says. "I . . . speak as a creative artist, and not as a critic." The creative artist, he remarks, on another occasion, produces "the finest, and the only first-rate criticism".

We do not think that this is a book of first-rate criticism; but it is the book of an artist. Nobody could read one of these short little papers without feeling himself in the presence of the father of fifty volumes. The man who speaks knows all that there is to be known about the making of books. He remembers that a tremendous amount of work has gone to the making of them; he is versed in every side of the profession—agents and publishers, good seasons and bad seasons, the size of editions and the size of royalties, he knows it all— he loves it all. He never affects to despise the business side of the profession of writing. He will talk of high-class stuff, thinks that authors are quite right in getting every cent they can for it, and will remark that it is the business of a competent artist to please, if not *the*, certainly *a*, public. But it is not in this sense only that he is far more professional than the English writer is apt to be or to appear; he is professional in his demand that a novel shall be made absolutely seaworthy and well constructed. If he hates one sin more than another it is the sin of "intellectual sluggishness". This is not the attitude nor are these the words of "mandarins" or "dilettanti"—the professors and the cultivated people whom Mr Bennett hates much as the carpenter hates the amateur who does a little fretwork.

London swarms with the dilettanti of letters. They do not belong to the criminal classes, but their good intentions, their culture, their judiciousness, and their infernal cheek amount perhaps to worse than arson or assault. . . . They shine at tea, at dinner, and after dinner. They talk more easily than [the artist] does, and write more easily too. They can express themselves more readily. And they know such a deuce of a lot.

Whether we agree or disagree we are reminded by this healthy outburst of rage that the critic has not merely to deal out skilfully measured doses of praise and blame to individuals, but to keep the atmosphere in a right state for the production of works of art. The atmosphere, even seven years ago, was in a state so strange that it appears almost fantastic now. Canon Lambert was then saying, "I would just as soon send a daughter of mine to a house infected with diphtheria or typhoid fever as" let her read *Ann Veronica*. About the same time Dr Barry remarked, "I never leave my house . . . but I am forced to see, and solicited to buy, works flamingly advertised of which the gospel is adultery and the apocalypse the right of suicide." We must be very grateful to Mr Bennett for the pertinacity with which he went on saying in such circumstances "that the first business of a work of art is to be beautiful, and its second not to be sentimental".

But if we were asked to give a proof that Mr Bennett is something more than the extremely competent, successful, businesslike producer of literature, we would point to the paper on "Neo-Impressionism and Literature". These new pictures, he says, have wearied him of other pictures; is it not possible that some writer will come along and do in words what these men have done in paint? And suppose that happens, and Mr Bennett has to admit that he has been concerning himself unduly with inessentials, that he has been worrying himself to achieve infantile realisms? He will admit it, we are sure; and that he can ask himself such a question seems to us certain proof that he is what he claims to be—a "creative artist".

Mr Galsworthy's Novel

Review of *Beyond*, by John Galsworthy. (30 August, 1917.)

EVERYONE, especially in August, especially in England, can bring to mind the peculiar mood which follows a long day of exercise in the open air. The body is tired out; the mind washed smooth by countless gallons of fresh air, and for some reason everything seems dangerously simple, and the most complex and difficult decisions obvious and inevitable. There is something truly or falsely spiritual about this state, and it is one which if prolonged may easily lead to disaster. In Mr Galsworthy's new novel the people fill us with alarm, because they appear all more or less under the influence of the great narcotic and therefore not quite responsible for their actions. They have been out hunting all day for so many generations that they are now perpetually in this evening condition of physical well-being and spiritual simplicity. With minds one blur of field and lane, hounds and foxes, they make sudden and tremendous decisions marked by the peculiar lightness and boldness of those who are drugged out of self-consciousness by the open air. Just before they drop off to sleep they decide that they must get married tomorrow, or elope with a housemaid, or challenge someone to fight a duel. This, of course, is an exaggeration, but some theory of the kind must be fabricated to explain this rather queer book, *Beyond*.

Charles Clare Winton, a major in the Lancers, was evidently in the condition described when he fell in love and had a child by a lady who was already the wife of a country squire, his friend. Nothing was more against all his ideas and, what is more important in the case of Major Winton, his tradition of good breeding than such behaviour. The child, a girl called Gyp, was left to his guardianship by the unsuspecting squire; and he salved his conscience to some extent by looking after her affairs and improving her investments. She lived with him and took his name. Being his daughter she was naturally extremely well-bred, loved dogs, and rode like a bird; but being a woman, very attractive, in an ambiguous position, and endowed with a passion for music, her lot was evidently to be complicated by queer sudden impulses on the part of others besides those which she felt for herself. At her first dance she was kissed on the elbow; by the time she was twenty-two she was involved in an affair with a long-haired Swedish violinist, called Fiorsen, whom she met when her father went to take the waters at Wiesbaden. In a second, as it seems to our apprehensive eyes, she is embraced by him; next minute she is actually married to a man whose past has been disreputable, and whom her father dislikes. "That long, loping, wolfish, fiddling fellow with the broad cheek bones and little side whiskers (good God!) and greenish eyes, whose looks at Gyp he secretly marked down, roused his complete distrust." But he was a man of few words, and his own experience of love had convinced him that it was useless to interfere. The alarming thing was that Gyp herself had never given the matter any serious thought; her talks with Fiorsen, in spite of the embraces, had been of the most elementary and formal description. For example, coming home "bone-tired" from a long day's hunting, she hears that Fiorsen is in the house; she has a hot bath and does for a moment consider what will happen if she refuses him. ". . . The thought staggered her. Had she, without knowing it, got so far as this? Yes, and further. It was all no good. Fiorsen would never accept refusal even if she gave it. But, did she want to refuse? She loved hot baths, but had never stayed in one so long. Life was so easy there, and so difficult outside." She was not in love with Fiorsen; the only serious element in her decision was that, according to a certain Baroness, Fiorsen wanted saving from himself; and the task appealed to her. No wonder, then, that when she finds herself alone with her husband for the first time after the wedding, "she thought of her frock, a mushroom coloured velvet cord".

From these quotations it is not possible, perhaps, to gather that Mr Galsworthy is giving Gyp his closest and most serious attention. He represents her not only as a very finely organized being, fastidious, sensitive, and proud, but she lives her life and meets the harsh and inevitable blows of fate by a code of morality which has Mr Galsworthy's respect. It is by this time a matter of course that whatever Mr Galsworthy respects we must take seriously; whatever story he writes is likely to be not merely a story but also a point of view. But this time we must admit that we have not been able to get ourselves into that sympathetic state in which we read if not with agreement still with conviction. At every crisis in Gyp's fate, instead of feeling that the laws of society have forced her into positions where her passion and her courage vindicate her behaviour completely, we feel that she acts without enough thought to realize what she is doing—and therefore callously and conventionally; without enough passion to carry her triumphantly "beyond". She never forgets what the servants will think; and at a terrible moment she can remember that she is walking down Baker-street without any gloves on and can forget her emotion in buying a pair. Behind her behaviour there is no code of morality; there is only a standard of manners which she was taught, no doubt, by the charming maiden aunt who lives in Curzon-street. This, of course, would be all very well if there were any trace of satire or of protest in Mr Galsworthy's portrait of her and her surroundings; but there is none. If you try to read the book as a satire upon honourable officers in the Lancers who hunt all day and sleep all night, to see in Gyp an amiable and innocent girl who has been flung disastrously from her dogs and ponies to sink or swim in the whirlpool of the world without any weapon save good manners, you are painfully at cross-purposes with your author. Gyp, he is careful to point out, is neither a "new woman", nor is she a "society woman"; she is a woman of temperament, of refinement, and of courage. And we are asked to believe that in the great things of life she was carried "beyond" other people, and that these weapons of hers were good enough to fight her battles very finely, and to leave her in the end mistress of her soul and able to say, although her heart is broken and she can only find comfort in a Home for Poor Children, "I wouldn't have been without it".

There are many other characters in the book, but they have, unfortunately, as we think, to comply with the standard which Gyp accepts. Fiorsen and Rosek are men of rather unpleasant character; Summerhay is a man of rather pleasant character. Gyp sums him up very well by her remark: "I like men who think first of their dogs." Unfortunately she is led to exclaim more than once in the book also, "What animals men are!" Did she give them a chance, we wonder, of being anything much better? But the whole society seems to us to have had its sting, whether for good or for evil, for happiness or unhappiness, drawn long ago, and to be living rather a colourless than a vicious or beautiful life. There is nothing coarse or boisterous about this world; nobody seems to want anything very much, and when we think it all over at the end we remember, and this we mean sincerely and not satirically, a great many most delightful dogs.

Philosophy in Fiction

Review of *Writings by L. P. Jacks*. (10 January, 1918.)

AFTER one has heard the first few bars of a tune upon a
barrel organ the further course of the tune is instinctively foretold by the mind and any deviation from that
pattern is received with reluctance and discomfort. A
thousand tunes of the same sort have grooved a road in our
minds and we insist that the next tune we hear shall flow
smoothly down the same channels; nor are we often dis-
obeyed. That is also the case with the usual run of stories.
From the first few pages you can at least half-consciously
foretell the drift of what is to follow, and certainly a part
of the impulse which drives us to read to the end comes
from the desire to match our foreboding with the fact. It is
not strange then that the finished product is much what we
expected it to be, and bears no likeness, should we compare
it with reality, to what we feel for ourselves. For loudly
though we talk of the advance of realism and boldly though
we assert that life finds its mirror in fiction, the material of
life is so difficult to handle and has to be limited and abstrac-
ted to such an extent before it can be dealt with by words that
a small pinch of it only is made use of by the lesser novelist.
He spends his time moulding and remoulding what has
been supplied him by the efforts of original genius perhaps
a generation or two ago. The moulds are by this time so
firmly set, and require such effort to break them, that the
public is seldom disturbed by explosions in that direction.

These reflections arise when we try to account for the
discomfort which so often afflicts us in reading the works of
Mr Jacks. We do not insinuate that he is therefore a great
writer; he has not increased the stock of our knowledge very
largely, nor has he devised a shape which seems completely
satisfactory for his contributions; but nevertheless he is
disconcerting. In the first place he has one distinction which
we wish that more novelists shared with him, the distinction
of being something besides a novelist. His bias towards
philosophy and religious speculation leads him off the high

road and carries him to blank spaces where the path has
not been cut nor the name chosen. He is an explorer, and
in view of that fact we can forgive him some wanderings
which seem to lead nowhere and others which end, as far as
our eyesight serves us, in a fog. We fancy that he reverses
some of the common methods of those who write fiction.
More often than not the seed which the novelist picks up and
brings to flower is dropped in some congregation of human
beings, from sayings, gestures, or hints; but we should guess
that Mr Jacks most commonly finds his seed between the
pages of a book, and the book is quite often a book of
philosophy. That at once gives him a different method of
approach and a different direction. He is acquainted with
Moral Science: he looks up from the page and wonders
what would happen should some of its doctrines be put into
practice. He conceives an undergraduate and sets him the
task of atoning for the sins of a dissolute father according to
the teachings he has learnt in the schools. The crisis of the
story therefore takes the form of a philosophical argument
between two undergraduates as to the morality of giving a
shilling to a tramp, and the one who proves his case shall
marry the lady. It seems to us extremely unlikely that anyone could hum the rest of that tune from hearing the first
few bars. It is plain that if you are ordering your imaginary
universe from this angle your men and women will have to
adapt themselves to dance to a new measure. The criticism
which will rise to the lips of every reader who finds himself
put out by the unwonted sight is that the characters have
ceased to be "real" or "alive" or "convincing". But let him
make sure that he is looking at life and not at the novelist's
dummy. Or he might do worse than reflect whether likeness
to life is the prime merit in a novel; and, if that is agreed
upon, whether life is not a much more ubiquitous presence
than one is led by the novelist to suppose. Whether or not
Mr Jacks has discovered a new vein of the precious stuff,
some rare merit must be allowed a writer who through five
volumes of stories lures us on to the last word of the last page.

He causes us to remember the exhilaration of driving by
dusk when one cannot foresee the ups or the downs of the
road. With Mr Jacks starting his story anywhere, following

it anywhere and leaving it anywhere, as he is in the habit of doing, the incentive of the unexpected is constantly supplied to us. "Oh, I'm nobody in particular," he remarks in *A Grave Digger's Scene*. "Just passing through and taking a look round"; and anything that his eye lights upon may start a story, which story may be a parable, or a satire upon religious sects, or a ghost story, or a straightforward study of a farmer's character, or a vision, or an argument, with figures merely put in as pegs to mark the places. But although he disregards all the rules and effects a most arbitrary tidying up when he remembers them, there is one invariable partner in all his enterprises—a keen and educated intelligence.

Intelligence, with its tendency to acquire views and its impatience with the passive attitude of impartial observation, may be a source of danger in fiction should it get the upper hand; but even in a state of subjection it is so rare that we must welcome it on its own terms. The only reservation which we feel disposed to make in the case of Mr Jacks' intelligence is that it fills his mind too full with ideas derived from other sources to give him a wide and unprejudiced view of his subject. Instead of going on with his tale, he has views upon Socialism, or sex problems, or education, or psychology which must be brought in and investigated at the expense of the individual. But even this reservation must be qualified. The portraits of Farmer Perryman, Farmer Jeremy and Peter Rodright have the stuff in them of three-volume novels, and give the essence of different types without deviation into the mystical or the abnormal. On account of their solid truth we prefer them to the study of Snarley Bob in *Mad Shepherds*, whose portrait seems to have been made up from some cunning prescription found in the books rather than from direct observation. Yet as we make this criticism we are aware that it may merely represent the shudder of a conservative mind forced to consider what it has always shunned, invited to land upon one of the "Desolate Islands" not marked upon the map. Expectancy mingles itself in equal proportions with our distrust, for the things that Mr Jacks tries to bring into the light are among the deepest and the most obscure. "Things from the abyss of time that float upwards into dreams—sleeping things whose breath sometimes breaks the surface of our waking consciousness, like bubbles rising from the depths of Lethe."

Inevitably it is extremely difficult to combine these new trophies of psychology with the old; and the results are often queer composite beings, monsters of a double birth, fit for the museum rather than the breakfast table. When, among other curiosities, we read of a mare which has mysteriously acquired the personality of a professor's lost love we can hardly help remarking, "Piecraft is trying to live in two worlds, the world of imagination and the world of pure science; he will come to grief in both of them." But if we are more often interested than moved by Mr Jacks's stories, the balance is so seldom on that side that it would be churlish to demand a combination which only the very few can give us. For some reason or other intelligence is particularly rare in fiction. At first sight it seems that there must be something amiss with a story which is aimed at the reason; when we find sentence after sentence brief, pointed and expressive we shiver at a nakedness that seems momentarily indecent. But when we have rid ourselves of a desire for the dusky draperies of fiction there is no small pleasure in being treated neither as child nor as sultan, but as an equal and reasonable human being. Mr Jacks uniformly achieves this wholesome result by writing with an exactness which gives a sharp idea of his meaning. Nothing is modified out of deference to our laziness. And occasionally, as in the remarkable paper called *The Castaway*, he writes what we may read not only for the light which it casts upon his methods, but for its own rare beauty. We quote the last passage:

Desolate Islands, more than I could ever explore, more than I could count or name, I found in the men and women who press upon me every day. Nay, my own life was full of them; the flying moment was one; they rose out of the deep with the ticking of the clock. And once came the rushing of a mighty wind; and the waves fled backward till the sea was no more. Then I saw that the Islands were great mountains uplifted from everlasting foundations, their basis one beneath the ocean floor, their summits many above the sundering waters—most marvellous of all the works of God.

The Green Mirror

Review of *The Green Mirror*, by Hugh Walpole. (24 January, 1918.)

IN the drawing-room, over the mantelpiece, there hung a green mirror. Many generations of the Trenchard family had seen themselves reflected in its depths. Save for themselves and for the reflection of themselves they had never seen anything else for perhaps three hundred years, and in the year 1902 they were still reflected with perfect lucidity. If there was any room behind the figures for chair or table, tree or field, chairs, tables, trees and fields were now and always had been the property of the Trenchard family. It is impossible to limit the pride of this family in itself.

> Not to be a Trenchard was to be a nigger or a Chinaman.... The Trenchards had never been conceited people—conceit implied too definite a recognition of other people's position and abilities. To be conceited you must think yourself abler, more interesting, richer, handsomer than some one else—and no Trenchard ever realized anyone else.

The reader who is acquainted with modern fiction will at this point reflect that he has met these people or their relations already; they must belong to that composite group of English families created by Mr Galsworthy, Mr Arnold Bennett and Mr E. M. Forster. Very different in detail, they all share a common belief that there is only one view of the world, and one family; and invariably at the end the mirrors break, and the new generation bursts in.

This is said more in order to describe Mr Walpole's novel than to criticize it, although it is by this door that criticism will enter. There is no fault to be found with the theme. If the family theme has taken the place of the love theme with our more thoughtful writers, that goes to prove that for this generation it is the more fertile of the two. It has so many sides to it, like all living themes, that there is no reason why one book should repeat another. You may destroy the family and salute the dawn by any means at your disposal, passion, satire, or humour, provided that you are in love with your cause. But the danger of a cause which has had great exponents lies in its power to attract recruits who are converts to other people's reforms but are not reformers themselves. In so far as Mr Walpole presents the Trenchard family as a type of the pig-headed British race with its roots in the past and its head turned backwards he seems to us to fail. The place for the Trenchard type is the didactic stage. All the exaggerations of their insularity would hit the mark delivered from the mouths of actors, but from the mouths of people in a book with the merits of this book they sound forced and unreal. "It was one of the Trenchard axioms that any one who crossed the English Channel conferred a favour"; no Trenchard can marry a man who thinks "Russia such a fine country". And quite in keeping with the limelight is the Uncle's well-known lecture upon the approaching break-up of his class. "Nearly the whole of our class in England has, ever since the beginning of last century, been happily asleep. . . . Oh, young Mark's just one of the advance guard. He's smashing up the Trenchards with his hammer the same way that all the families like us up and down England are being smashed up." The hammer is thrown and the mirror comes down with a crash. Upstairs a very old Mr Trenchard falls back dead; and out we pour into the street looking askance at the passers-by as though we ought to tell them too that another English family has been smashed to splinters and freedom is stealing over the roof-tops.

Mr Walpole's gift is neither for passion nor for satire, but he possesses an urbane observant humour. He has a true insight into the nature of domesticity. He can render perfectly the "friendly confused smell of hams and medicine, which is the Stores note of welcome". The psychology of a lady charged with the exciting duty of buying three hot-water bottles is no secret to him. We have seldom met a better account of a long Sunday in the country and the cold supper with which it ends. On this occasion the servants were out, and there was no soup. These are the small things in which Mr Walpole is invariably happy, and in our view it is no disparagement to a writer to say that his gift is for the small things rather than for the large. Scott was master

THE GREEN MIRROR

of the large method, but Jane Austen was mistress of the small. If you are faithful with the details the large effects will grow inevitably out of those very details. In its way the portrait of the hobbledehoy brother Henry is a large achievement, based though it is upon a careful study of hot-water bottles and Sunday suppers. The aunts, too, when they are not drawn violently from their orbits by the young man who has spent some years in Moscow, prattle, squabble, and make it up again in the warm soft atmosphere of true imagination. There is no reason for Mr Walpole to apologize for what is slow, uneventful, and old-fashioned in the world which he portrays. We feel convinced that in these respects the war has done nothing to change it. The Trenchard family, far from having sprung apart when the mirror was unfortunately broken, had it mended at an expensive shop in Bond-street, and it was hanging as usual over the mantelpiece on August 4, 1914. Mrs Trenchard never did anything so hysterical as to turn her daughter from her house because she married a young man who talked rather superficially about Russia. Mother and daughter are at this moment knitting comforters together. The only person who turned out badly, as Mrs Trenchard said he would, was Mr Philip Mark—but it is no business of ours to write other people's novels. We confess that in this case we should like to, but that is only because Mr Walpole has done it in many respects so extremely well himself.

Moments of Vision

Review of *Trivia*, by Logan Pearsall Smith. (23 May, 1918.)

TO some readers the very sight of a book in which the plain paper so generously balances the printed paper will be a happy omen. It seems to foretell gaiety, ease, unconcern. Possibly the writer has written to please himself. He has begun and left off and begun again as the mood seized him. Possibly he has had a thought for our pleasure. At any rate, our attention is not going to be stretched on the rack of an extended argument. Here is a handful of chosen flowers, a dinner of exquisite little courses, a bunch of variously coloured air balloons. Anticipating pleasure of this rare kind from the fact that Mr Pearsall Smith's *Trivia* seldom do more than reach the bottom of the page and sometimes barely encroach upon its blankness, we deserve to be disappointed. We deserve to find moral reflections or hints for the economical management of the home. Perhaps our unblushing desire for pleasure of itself deserves to be disappointed. We can fancy that many of Mr Pearsall Smith's readers will placate their consciences for the sin of reading him by some excuse about going to bed or getting up. There are times, they will say, when it is impossible to read anything serious.

It is true that there is little to be got from this book except pleasure. It has no mission, it contains no information, unless you can dignify with that name the thoughts that come into the head, buzz through it, and go out again without improving the thinker or adding to the wealth of the world. The head of the author of *Trivia* contains, as he confesses, a vast store of book learning; but his thoughts have little serious concern with that; they may light upon some obscure folio as a robin might perch for a moment upon a book before flitting to the marble bust of Julius Caesar and so on to the shining brass head of the poker and tongs. This lightness, more justly to be compared to the step of a crane among wild flowers, is perhaps the first thing you notice. The second is that although Mr Pearsall Smith has preserved the freshness and idiosyncrasy of his idea he has done so by the unostentatious use of great literary skill. Nor can we long overlook the fact that his purpose is as serious as the purpose that fulfils itself in other books of more ambitious appearance. If we are not mistaken, it is his purpose to catch and enclose certain moments which break off from the mass, in which without bidding things come together in a combination of inexplicable significance, to arrest those thoughts which suddenly, to the thinker at least, are almost menacing with meaning. Such moments of vision are of an unaccountable nature; leave them alone and they persist for years; try to explain them and they disappear; write them down and they die beneath the pen.

One of the reasons which has led to Mr Pearsall Smith's success is that he has taken neither himself nor his thoughts too seriously. Most people would have been tempted to fill the blank pages. They would have strained to be more profound, more brilliant, or more emphatic. Mr Pearsall Smith keeps well on this side of comfort; he knows exactly how far his gift will carry him. He is on easy terms with what he calls "that Masterpiece of Nature, a reason-endowed and heaven-facing Man". "What stellar collisions and conflagrations, what floods and slaughters and enormous efforts has it not cost the Universe to make me—of what astral periods and cosmic processes am I not the crown and wonder?" Nevertheless, he is conscious of belonging to that sub-order of the animal kingdom which includes the orang-outang, the gorilla, the baboon, and the chimpanzee. His usual mood towards himself and towards the rest of us is one of ironic but affectionate detachment, befitting an elderly Pierrot conscious of grey hairs. The poplar tree delights him and the "lemon-coloured moon". "After all these millions of years, she ought to be ashamed of herself!" he cries out, beholding the "great amorous unabashed face of the full moon." As he listens to the talk of the thoughtful baronet:

I saw the vast landscape of the world, dim, as in an eclipse; its population eating their bread with tears, its rich men

sitting listless in their palaces, and aged Kings crying,"Vanity,
Vanity, all is Vanity!" laboriously from their thrones. . . .
When I seek out the sources of my thoughts, I find that they
had their beginning in fragile chance; were born of little
moments that shine for me curiously in the past. . . . So I never
lose a chance of the whimsical and perilous charm of daily
life, with its meetings and words and accidents. Why, to-day,
perhaps, or next week, I may hear a voice, and, packing up
my Gladstone bag, follow it to the ends of the world.

The voice may be the voice of Beauty, but all the same he
does not forget to pack his Gladstone bag. Compared with
the "whimsical and perilous charm of daily life", compared
with the possibility that one of these days one may discover
the right epithet for the moon, are not all the ends of serious
middle-aged ambition "only things to sit on"?

We have marked a number of passages for quotation,
but as it would be necessary to quote them only in part we
refrain. But the mark was not in the margin of the book;
a finger seemed to raise itself here and there as if to exclaim,
"At last! It has been said." And, without making extra-
vagant claims for a gift which would certainly refuse to bear
a weight of honour, to cut these passages into two or otherwise mutilate them would be to damage a shape so fitting
and so characteristic that we can fancy these small craft
afloat for quite a long time, if not in mid stream, still in
some very pleasant backwater of the river of immortality.

Mr Merrick's Novels

Review of *While Paris Laughed* and *Conrad in Quest of his Youth.*
(4 July, 1918.)

TWELVE distinguished authors "have fallen over each other," says Sir James Barrie, "in their desire to join in the honour of writing the prefaces" to the edition of Mr Merrick's collected works. At the present moment only the first of the twelve, Sir James Barrie, has appeared in the capacity of introducer, and he is in charge of *Conrad in Quest of his Youth.* Sir James, we need not say, makes the introduction in the most graceful terms, and leaves us to become better acquainted with the genial assurance that we shall get on splendidly; but, should it fall out otherwise, it will make no difference to his opinion of Mr Merrick. "For long he has been the novelist's novelist, and we give you again the chance to share him with us; you have been slow to take the previous chances, and you may turn away again, but in any case he will still remain our man." To start us on the right track he gives it as his opinion that *Conrad in Quest of his Youth* "is the best sentimental journey that has been written in this country since the publication of the other one". To leave us in no possible doubt of his meaning he adds, "I know scarcely a novel by any living Englishman, except a score or so of Mr Hardy's, that I would rather have written."

The reader, thus advised and admonished, bethinks him perhaps of the *Sentimental Journey*, conjures up the name of any novel by a living author that he might choose to have written, and conjectures that Mr Merrick will be first and foremost an artist whose gift has a rarity that specially appeals to connoisseurs. We maintain that this is the wrong way of approaching Mr Merrick. When Sir James suggests Sterne, when he talks of Mr Hardy, he is challenging us to make comparisons which we would much rather make in silence. He is putting us into the ungrateful position of the critic whose main business it is to find fault. Now the interest and value of the art of criticism lie more than anything in the critic's ability to seize upon what is good and to expati-

ate upon that. The only criticism worth having, we sometimes think, is the criticism of praise; but to give praise its
meaning the standard of the first rate must be present in the
mind, unconfused and unlowered, though kept in the background unless the merit of the work makes open reference
to it worth while. Rightly or wrongly we cannot see that
there is anything to be gained by naming the classics when
we are discussing the interesting but unequal works of Mr
Merrick.

Conrad in Quest of his Youth is an extremely readable book.
More than that, it is sufficiently unlike other books to make
you wish to take its measure, to account for its failure or its
success. Here, evidently, is a novelist endowed with wit,
with lightness of touch, with a sensitive quick-darting
intelligence, and with just that turn of mind that is needed
to give his work an unmistakable character of its own.
Perhaps this last is the quality that has endeared him to his
fellow writers. It is very rare, and yet, if unsupported by
commoner gifts, it is apt to be thrown away, or at least completely ignored by the public. Competence, completeness
and a dozen other virtues are negligible compared with the
sensitive though perhaps ineffective handling of the artist.
Within his limits Mr Merrick shows unmistakable traces of
this endowment. Is not *Conrad in Quest of his Youth* an undoubted proof of it? From a dozen different scenes, pre-
cariously poised one on top of another, we get a charming
irregular whole; we get a sense of the past; of deserted piers,
of bathing places out of season, of barrel organs out of tune,
of ladies past their prime. It has an atmosphere of its own.
Mr Merrick possesses the cynicism peculiar to the senti-
mentalist; and in *Conrad* the mixture is extremely skilful,
the sweet turning bitter, the sunset merging surprisingly
into the daylight of three o'clock in the afternoon. His
talent seems to lend itself peculiarly well to the faded distinction of the year 1880, when Piccadilly was blocked with
hansom cabs and well-dressed people sat by Rotten Row
and offered each other nicely turned phrases which already
sound a little obsolete. Here is an example of this urbane
dialogue; Conrad is talking to the lady whom he loved in his
youth:

"You hurt me," said Conrad, "because for the first time I realize you are different from the girl I've looked for. Till now I've felt that I was with her again." "That's nice of you, but it isn't true. Oh, I like you for saying it, of course. . . . If you had felt it really—" "Go on." "No; what for? I should only make you unhappier." "You want comedy?" he demurred; "you have said the saddest things a woman ever said to me!" She raised a white shoulder—with a laugh. "I never get what I want!" "It should have taught you to feel for me, but you are not 'wondrous kind.' " "Oh, I am more to be pitied than you are! What have I got in my life? Friends? Yes—to play bridge with. My husband? He delivers speeches on local option, and climbs mountains. Both make me deadly tired. I used to go in for music—'God Save the King' is the only tune he knows when he hears it, and he only knows that because the men take their hats off. I was interested in my house at the beginning— after you've quarrelled in your house every day for years it doesn't absorb you to make the mantelpiece look pretty. I wanted a child—well, my sister has seven! . . . Voilà my auto- biography up to date." "There is tomorrow," said Conrad, moved. "To-morrow you must give me the comedy," she smiled. . . .

There is much that is up to that level, a good deal that is above it, and as his books are full of dialogue you may accuse Mr Merrick of airiness, perhaps of emptiness, but never of being a bore.

The success of *Conrad in Quest of his Youth* lies in the skilful balance of sweetness and bitterness, of romance and reality. But in the other novels the union is far more unequal, and in some of them the results appear to us to be more interest- ing. We can guess that Mr Merrick has tried, as most good novelists try, to shape a world bearing some resemblance to the world of his vision. Failure, the loss of ideals, the sacri- fice of good to evil, and, above all, the degradation wrought upon the character by poverty, were some of the aspects of life that claimed Mr Merrick's attention. He did not master his theme, and perhaps he spoilt a book or two in trying; but it is evident that he was not content with a scene of bril- liancy here, a character of vitality there, but aimed at

something more complete. If you choose, as this characteristic makes it possible, to consider his books as one large
composition, you must place in the centre a blazing fire, a
radiance that casts its fictitious splendour to the furthest
corners of the picture. This, of course, is the Stage. Into
that fire, from distant and obscure sources, come running
heroes and heroines and other strange figures, who struggle
to the light and pass out again into the dreary twilight of
failure or disillusion, or remain hovering unsatisfied at a
distance. And now we reach the dilemma by which Mr
Merrick seems so often to have been posed. He feels the
glamour of the stage in every nerve, he thrusts his men and
women again and again into the furnace, but then at the
last moment he repents and saves them alive. He bestows all
sorts of gifts upon them. This one turns out to be a successful
dramatist; that one earns £4,000 a year by painting pictures
which are, incredibly enough, works of the highest merit.
We do not believe with Sir James Barrie that Mr Merrick
has frightened the public by his pessimism; we think it more
probable that he has puzzled it by his compromises. His
mediocrity is so strangely combined with his excellence.
We have always to reckon with a lapse into melodrama as
in the ending to *The Man who was Good*, or with the commonplace and conventional as in the climax of *The House of
Lynch*.

But we own to a grudge against the influence that has
tried to spoil *Peggy Harper* or *The Quaint Companions*, because,
pruned of certain weaknesses, each of these books contains
first-hand truth seized and set down with extraordinary
vivacity. The proximity of the stage always revives Mr
Merrick, and a second-rate actress never fails to put him on
his mettle. Her cheap prettiness, her artistic incompetence,
her vanity, her courage, her poverty, her makeshifts and
artifices and endurance, together with the seduction of the
theatre, are described not with mere truth of detail,
though we guess that to be considerable, but with the rarer
truth of sympathy. The description of Peggy Harper's home
and of her mother, the decayed actress who has taken to
drink but preserves the artistic instincts and passions,
makes you feel that you have learned the truth about that

section of humanity once for all. From each of Mr Merrick's books one could select a chapter or two possessing, often among second-rate surroundings, this stamp of first-hand quality. We find it most often when he has to deal with the seamy side of the stage; we find it oddly often in some minor character or in some little scene dashed off apparently by an afterthought. A touring company comes to grief, a girl stumbling through her part before the author, a troupe of actors trailing their draggled feathers and cheap tinsel across the windy parade of a seaside resort at Christmas time—into such scenes he puts so much spirit, so many quick touches of insight, that the precarious, flaring, tenth-rate life of the provincial stage has not only glamour and bustle, but beauty into the bargain. These are the scenes that we shall wish to read again.

The last of Mr Merrick's books, *While Paris Laughed*, should win a greater popularity than the others. Nothing in it is so good as certain passages that we should have liked to quote, from *Peggy Harper* in particular, but the quality is far more equal. It has all the quickness, lightness, and dexterity which scarcely ever fail him, and, in addition, the balance of this uneven talent is more successfully maintained. In recording the adventures of the poet Tricotrin in Paris he is never quite serious, but he never laughs aloud; he hints at disagreeables and glances at delights; he suggests the divinity of art and the obtuseness of the public, but never for an instant does he pass from raillery to satire, or from suggestion to statement. It is a very skilful and craftsmanlike piece of work, and, if Mr Merrick still remains unpopular, we confess ourselves unable to guess the reason.

The "Movie" Novel

Review of *The Early Life and Adventures of Sylvia Scarlett*, by
Compton Mackenzie. (29 August, 1918.)

WHEN we say that the adventures of Sylvia Scarlett
are much more interesting than Sylvia Scarlett herself,
we are recommending the book to half the reading public
and condemning it in the eyes of the other half. There are
people who require the heroines of their novels to be interesting, and they know by experience that the adventurous
heroine is apt to be as dull in fiction as she is in life. It is true
that adventurers are not dull in the ordinary sense of the
word; they are monotonous, self-centred, serious, rather
than dull. They have spun all their substance into adventure, and nothing remains of them but a frail shell inhabited
by a very small creature with an enormous egotism and an
overweening vanity. The charge may be just, yet there is a
great deal to be said in praise of adventures themselves, and
not a little relief in finding occasionally that people are not
quite so interesting as writers are in the habit of insisting,
in novels, that we shall find them. Perhaps Sylvia might
have been interesting if she had ever had the time to set
about it. She had her moments of introspection, as upon
that occasion when she announced "I represent the original
conception of the Hetaera—the companion. I don't want
to be made love to, and every man who makes love to me I
dislike. If I ever do fall in love, I'll be a man's slave." But
perhaps she was aware that being interesting was not in her
line, as we are inclined to agree with her that it was not. At
any rate, this reflection occurs in a momentary lull, and
directly Mr Mackenzie catches her in the lazy pose of self
analysis he gives a crack of his whip and sends her flying, as
merrily as if she had never heard the word Hetaera, through
the next hoop.

We cannot begin even to count those hoops. They are so
many and so variously designed that a bare programme of
the entertainment or a catalogue of the actors' names would
fill perhaps a score of columns. In very early youth Sylvia
came to England dressed as a boy and christened Sylvester

to share the shifts and adventures of her father, an abscond-
ing clerk, in the shadier suburbs of London. From the
addresses of their lodgings and the names of their friends
the experienced reader who has read, among other books,
the novels of Dickens will gather what sort of life they led,
and will even be able to improvise a certain amount of the
conversation of Mrs Bullwinkle, Mrs Gowndry, Mr Monk-
ley, and General Dashwood of Tinderbox lane. But it is
better and simpler to rely entirely upon Mr Mackenzie.
He does it so fast and so deftly that merely to keep up with
him is quite enough strain upon the faculties. He not only
finds names for landladies, cabmen, mountebanks, actresses,
tenors, managers, schoolmistresses, Barons, clergymen,
natives of Brazil, and maiden ladies living in villas appro-
priately named too, but he provides them with queer occu-
pations, and clever things to say, let alone a number of
surprising things to do. You can scarcely open the book
anywhere without finding a cab bolting down Haverstock-
hill with an eloping couple inside it, or a baboon escaping
from Earl's Court Exhibition, or an actor dropping dead, or
a curtain going up, or a landlady being funny. Here is a
shop incident to show how quickly it rattles along:

> The confusion in the shop became general: Mr Gonner cut
> his thumb, and the sight of the blood caused a woman who
> was eating a sausage to choke; another customer took advan-
> tage of the row to snatch a side of bacon and try to escape,
> but another customer with a finer moral sense prevented him;
> a dog, who was sniffing in the entrance, saw the bacon on the
> floor and tried to seize it, but, getting his tail trodden upon by
> somebody, he took fright and bit a small boy who was waiting
> to change a shilling into coppers. Meanwhile Sylvia . . .
> jumped on to the first omnibus, &c., &c.

When we reached this point we seized the opportunity,
not so much of being bored as of being out of breath, to
reflect upon the propriety after all of using the word adventure. It is true that Sylvia is left on top of an omnibus bound
for West Kensington without a penny in the world; she is
young, beautiful, and friendless into the bargain; we have
no idea what is going to become of her; why then do we

refuse to call it an adventure? The obvious way to settle the
question is to bring to mind Tom Jones, Moll Flanders,
Isopel Berners, or the Flaming Tinman. These people may
not be interesting either, but when any one of them has not
a penny in the world it is a serious matter. Compared with
Mr Mackenzie's characters they are a slow-moving race—
awkward, ungainly and simpleminded. But consider how
many things we know about them, how much we guess,
what scenes of beauty and romance we set them in, how
much of England is their background—without a word of
description perhaps, but merely because they are themselves. We can think about them when we are no longer
reading the book. But we cannot do this with Mr Mackenzie's characters; and the reason is, we fancy, that though
Mr Mackenzie can see them once he can never see them
twice, and, as in a cinema, one picture must follow another
without stopping, for if it stopped and we had to look at it we
should be bored. Now, it is a strange thing that no one has
yet been seen to leave a cinema in tears. The cab horse bolts
down Haverstock-hill and we think it a good joke; the
cyclist runs over a hen, knocks an old woman into the gutter,
and has a hose turned upon him. But we never care whether
he is wet or hurt or dead. So it is with Sylvia Scarlett and her
troupe. Up they get and off they go, and as for minding what
becomes of them, all we hope is that they will, if possible,
do something funnier next time. No, it is not a book of
adventures; it is a book of cinema.

Sylvia and Michael

Review of *Sylvia and Michael*, by Compton Mackenzie.
(20 March, 1919.)

THE feat that no reviewer of Mr Mackenzie's books can possibly attempt is to explain even in the most compressed form what happens. In *Sylvia and Michael* the reader must be content with the assurance that Sylvia Scarlett is, in the familiar phrase, "still running". We leave her, indeed seated upon the shore of a Greek island with her hand in the hand of Michael Fane: but figuratively speaking she is still running as hard as she can; and when the book is shut the eye of imagination sees her whisking over the skyline attended by the usual troupe of chorus girls and nondescript young men doing their best to keep up with her, but more and more hopelessly outdistanced by the speed of her legs and the astonishing volubility of her tongue. The number of volumes still to be run through we guess to be considerable. The race which ends in the Greek island begins in Petrograd and is continued under every condition of discomfort and danger, since not only is she periodically reduced to her last penny, but the European war is blazing and roaring all round her and never ceases to harry her and her companions much as a relentless mowing machine will drive all the small deer of a cornfield into the open.

The gifts which enable Mr Mackenzie to keep so large and various company in such incessant activity, at any rate of the legs, are not negligible, although whether they have anything to do with literature is an open question. They include, to begin with, an astonishing swiftness of eye, so that he has only to be in a room once in order to write a complete inventory of its furniture. And should the room be furnished not only with chairs and tables but with a large and queer assortment of men and women, he will with equal swiftness make an inventory of them too. He rattles off their little distinguishing peculiarities as if his fund were inexhaustible, and the out of the way nature of his discoveries stimulates the imagination to hold itself in readiness for a strange and delightful expedition. So, at an evening party, someone might whisper in your ear, "That lady is Mère Gontran, and she keeps owls in a shed, and when her collie barks she thinks it is the voice of her dead husband." One looks at Mère Gontran with an access of interest, and before the interest has died out someone else is introduced, who has some different peculiarity or even little trick of the hand such as plaiting four necklaces in a rope until the string breaks and the green shells fall on the floor, and what can be more natural than that the dogs should start fighting in the street at that moment, until someone throws a stone which hits one of them on the hind leg, so that he runs off leaving a trail of blood upon the pavement? Meanwhile, what has become of Mère Gontran? She is no longer there: we may keep on repeating to ourselves, "She keeps owls in a shed", but the light of that illumination is not everlasting.

But, though we own to have tried, it would be difficult to burlesque the extreme swiftness with which Mr Mackenzie whisks his figures across the stage. For the sake of such vivacity one is ready to pardon a considerable degree of superficiality. But since Sylvia is not whisked across the stage and has developed a habit of soliloquy in the intervals of activity it is difficult to account for our failure to find her when we come to look for her. But the more she talks the less we see her. "This Promethean morality that enchains the world and sets its bureaucratic eagle to gnaw the vitals of humanity," Sylvia cried, . . . "No, no it cannot be right to secure the many by debasing the few." That she says many smart things about war and religion and nationality is undeniable: but in the process of saying them she fades out of existence beyond the power of owl or necklace to revive her, and leaves us wondering why so clever a journalist should think it necessary to get himself up as a young woman. But what is it that this queer combination of movement and brilliancy, platitude and vacancy, reminds us of? Not in the least of Greek islands and besieged cities: but rather of an evening party where conversations are always being cut short, where people look queer in their finery, where great vivacity alternates with empty silences, and where it is the fate of some to be pinned in a corner and discoursed to eternally by a bore.

War in the Village

Review of *The Village Wife's Lament*, by Maurice Hewlett.
(12 September, 1918.)

NOWADAYS many whose minds have not been used to turn that way must stop and ponder what thoughts the country people carry with them to their work in the fields, or cogitate as they scrub the cottage floor. It is a matter for speculation and shyness since the gulf between the articulate and inarticulate is not to be crossed by facile questioning, and silence may seem after all the best we can offer by way of sympathy to people whose lives seem so mysteriously and for such ages steeped in silence. Thus Mr Hewlett has chosen one of the most difficult of tasks when he tries to think himself into the mind of the village wife, and to express thoughts "which she may never have formulated, but which, I am very sure, lie in her heart too deep for any utterance save that of tears". He has succeeded, beyond doubt, in writing a terse, moving, and very sincere poem; but that it is the lament of a village woman for her shepherd husband killed in France, and for the baby whose death followed upon his death, we are not so sure.

Yet it would be difficult to say what quality we seek for in Mr Hewlett's poem and find lacking. Where it would have been easy to offend there is no ground for offence; the conception is very dignified and as completely without a touch of the sentimentality, which the theme invites, as the language is almost equally free from the taint of the professional writer. The village wife has nothing idyllic about her. From her birth upwards she takes her share in what Mr Hewlett calls "the unending war" waged from one generation to another by the sons and daughters of the poor. She scrubs and rinses and milks the cows year in and year out.

On winter mornings dark and hard,
    White from aching bed,
There were the huddled fowls in yard
    All to be fed.
My frozen breath stream'd from my lips,

The cows were hid in steam;
I lost sense of my finger-tips
And milkt in a dream.

Very finely and truly Mr Hewlett bases her life deep down
among the roots of the earth; she grows among the other
growing things, and the hills and woods of her parish are
England and the world to her, and she has inherited from
generations of village women who lived this life and knew
its perils the morality upon which their lives were founded.

I learned at home the laws of Earth;
    The nest-law that says,
Stray not too far beyond the hearth,
    Keep truth always;
And then the law of sip and bite:
    Work, that there may be some
For you who crowd the board this night,
    And the one that is to come.
The laws are so for bird and beast,
    And so we must live:
They give the most who have the least,
    And gain of what they give.
For working women 'tis the luck,
    A child on the lap;
And when a crust he learn to suck,
    Another's for the pap.

This hard natural life scarcely shares in the changes of the
self-conscious world. It has grown so close to the earth and
so shaped itself to the laws of nature that it might well remain unshaken for ever. But one summer evening the
village wife hears one stranger say to another as he passes,
"Then that means war". From that moment her security is
troubled, and by November, to her inexpressible bewilderment, her own house and happiness are at the mercy of a
force so remote that, though it has power to take her husband from her, she can hardly figure to herself what the
nature of it is. Her husband feels it, and goes; more strangely
it takes not only his body, but makes unfamiliar all that she
knew in his spirit. She hears that he is missing, and exclaims:

Missing! My man had been dead
Before he went away.

What, then, remains for her? Nothing but to ask perpetually
those questions as to the reason and justice of these events
which in the mind of a woman who has placed her trust in
the rightness of the natural order have an extreme bitterness mixed with their bewilderment. She must puzzle out
why the world has deceived her; why her right was not right
after all.

The verses, as our quotations show, are plain, deeply felt,
and often beautiful. But, for all their scrupulous care and
regard for the truth, they strike us not so much as the
thoughts and laments of the woman herself as the words of a
very sympathetic spectator who is doing his best to express
what he supposes must be there beneath the silence and at
the heart of the tears. The argument has too much cogency,
the thoughts follow each other in too orderly a fashion to be
the cry of a woman bereft of husband and son. Perhaps it is
coarseness—the quality that is the most difficult of all for
the educated to come by—that is lacking. By coarseness we
mean something as far removed from vulgarity as can be.
We mean something vehement, full throated, carrying
down in its rush sticks and stones and fragments of human
nature pell-mell. That is what we miss in Mr Hewlett's
poem, fine though it is.

The Rights of Youth

Review of *Joan and Peter*, by H. G. Wells. (19 September, 1918.)

THE moralists of the nursery used to denounce a sin which went by the name of "talking at", and was rendered the more expressive by the little stress which always fell upon the "at", as if to signify the stabbing, jabbing, pinpricking nature of the sin itself. The essence of "talking at" was that you vented your irritation in an oblique fashion which it was difficult for your victim to meet otherwise than by violence. This old crime of the nursery is very apt to blossom afresh in people of mature age when they sit down to write a novel. It blossoms often as unconsciously as we may suppose that the pearl blossoms in the breast of the oyster. Unfortunately for art, though providentially for the moralist, the pearl that is produced by this little grain of rancour is almost invariably a sham one.

In the early chapters of *Joan and Peter* there are a great many scenes and characters which seem to have been secreted round some sharp-edged grain which fate has lodged in the sensitive substance of Mr Wells's brain. Lady Charlotte Sydenham had some such origin; so, too, had Miss Phoebe Stubland; the sketch of Arthur Stubland was due to a disturbance of the kind, and certainly the schoolmistresses of St George and the Venerable Bede had no other begetter. We catch ourselves wondering whether Mr Wells is any longer aware of the grotesque aspect of these figures of his, burdened as they are with the most pernicious or typical views of their decade, humped and loaded with them so that they can hardly waddle across the stage without coming painfully to grief. The conscientious reader will try to refer these burlesques to some such abstraction as the Anglican Church, or the vagaries of aimless and impulsive modernism in the eighteen-nineties; but if you are indolent you will be inclined to give up playing your part in the game of illusion, and to trifle with idle speculations as to the idiosyncrasies of Mr Wells. But soon the very crudeness of the satire leads us to make a distinction, and directly we are satisfied of its truth our irritation is spent and our interest aroused. Mr Wells is not irritated with these people personally, or he would have taken more pains to annoy them; he is irritated with the things they represent. Indeed, he has been so much irritated that he has almost forgotten the individual. He is sore and angry and exaggerated and abusive because the waste, the stupidity, the senility of our educational system have afflicted him as men are, for the most part, afflicted only by their personal calamities. He possesses the queer power of understanding that "the only wrongs that really matter to mankind are the undramatic general wrongs", and of feeling them dramatically, as if they had wronged him individually. Here, he says, we have two children endowed with everything that the world most needs, and let us see what the world will make of them. What education have we to offer them? What are we able to teach them about the three great questions of sex and State and religion? First, he gluts his rage upon Lady Charlotte and Miss Phoebe Stubland, much to the detriment of the book, and then the matter is seriously taken in hand by Mr Oswald Stubland, V.C., a gallant gentleman with imaginative views upon the British Empire. He had believed that the Empire was the instrument of world civilization, and that his duty in Central Africa was the duty of an enlightened schoolmaster. But when his health broke down he returned to the far more difficult task of educating two of the children of the Empire in the very metropolis of civilization. He started off upon a pilgrimage to the schools and colleges of England, asking imaginative questions, and getting more and more dismayed at the answers he received.

Don't you *know* that education is building up an imagination? I thought everybody knew that. . . . Why is he to *do* Latin? Why is he to *do* Greek? . . . What will my ward know about Africa when you have done with him? . . . Will he know anything about the way the Royal Exchange affects the Empire? . . . But why shouldn't he understand the elementary facts of finance?

This is a mere thimbleful from the Niagara which Mr Wells pours out when his blood is up. He throws off the trammels of fiction as lightly as he would throw off a coat in running a race. The ideas come pouring in whether he speaks them in his own person or lets Oswald have them, or quotes them from real books and living authorities, or invents and derides some who are not altogether imaginary. He does not mind what material he uses so long as it will stick in its place and is roughly of the shape and colour he wants. Fiction, you can imagine him saying, must take care of itself; and to some extent fiction does take care of itself. No one, at any rate, can make an inquiry of this sort so vivid, so pressing, so teeming and sprouting with suggestions and ideas and possibilities as he does; indeed, when he checks himself and exclaims, "But it is high time that Joan and Peter came back into the narrative," we want to cry out, "Don't bother about Joan and Peter. Go on talking about education." We have an uneasy suspicion that Joan and Peter will not be nearly so interesting as Mr Wells's ideas about their education and their destiny. But, after all, we know that Mr Wells is quite right when he says that it is time to bring them in. He would be shirking the most difficult part of his task if he left them out.

Like his own Oswald Stubland, Mr Wells "belongs to that minority of Englishmen who think systematically, whose ideas join on". He has "built up a sort of philosophy for himself", by which he does try his problems and with which he fits in such new ideas as come to him. He is not writing about education, but about the education of Joan and Peter. He is not isolating one of the nerves of our existence and tracing its course separately, but he is trying to give that nerve its place in the whole system and to show us the working of the entire body of human life. That is why his book attains its enormous bulk; and that is why, with all its sketchiness and crudeness and redundancy, its vast soft, billowing mass is united by a kind of coherency and has some relation to a work of art. If you could isolate the seed from which the whole fabric has sprung you would find it, we believe, to consist of a fiery passion for the rights of youth—a passion for courage, vitality, initiative, inventiveness, and all the qualities that Mr Wells likes best. And as Mr Wells can never think without making a picture of his thought, we do not have youth in the abstract, but Joan and Peter, Wilmington and Troop, Huntley and Hetty Reinhart. We have Christmas parties and dressings up and dances and night clubs and Cambridge and London and real people disguised under fictitious names, and very bright covers on the chairs and Post Impressionist pictures on the walls and advanced books upon the tables. This power of visualizing a whole world for his latest idea to grow in is the power that gives these hybrid books their continuity and vitality.

But because Mr Wells's ideas put on flesh and blood so instinctively and admirably we are able to come up close to them and look them in the face; and the result of seeing them near at hand is, as our suspicions assured us that it would be, curiously disappointing. Flesh and blood have been lavished upon them, but in crude lumps and unmodelled masses, as if the creator's hand, after moulding empires and sketching deities, had grown too large and slack and insensitive to shape the fine clay of men and women. It is curious to observe, for example, what play Mr Wells is now constrained to make with the trick of modernity. It is as if he suspected some defect in the constitution of his characters and sought to remedy it with rouge and flaxen wigs and dabs of powder, which he is in too great a hurry nowadays to fix on securely or plaster in the right places. But if Joan and Peter are merely masquerading rather clumsily at being the heirs of the ages, Mr Wells's passion for youth is no make-believe. The sacrifice, if we choose to regard it so, of his career as a novelist has been a sacrifice to the rights of youth, to the needs of the present moment, to the lives of the rising generation. He has run up his buildings to house temporary departments of the Government. But if he is one of those writers who snap their fingers in the face of the future, the roar of genuine applause which salutes every new work of his more than makes up, we are sure, for the dubious silence, and possibly the unconcealed boredom, of posterity.

Mr Hudson's Childhood

Review of *Far Away and Long Ago*, by W. H. Hudson.
(26 September, 1918.)

SINCE in this account of his childhood Mr Hudson speculates as to the origin of certain childish instincts, one may perhaps suitably begin what one has to say of his book by recalling a childish impression which his writing has brought to mind. Between or behind the dense and involved confusion which grown-up life presented there appeared for moments chinks of pure daylight in which the simple, unmistakable truth, the underlying reason, otherwise so overlaid and befogged, was revealed. Such seasons, or more probably seconds, were of so intense a revelation that the wonder came to be how the truth could ever again be overcast, as it certainly would be overcast directly this lantern-like illumination went out. Somehow or other Mr Hudson writes as if he held his lantern steadily upon this simple, unmistakable truth, and had never been deluded or puzzled or put off by the confusions which overlay it. It is an effect that the great Russian writers produce far more commonly than the English, and may perhaps be connected with the surroundings of their childhood, so different both for Mr Hudson and for the Russians from the surroundings of the ordinary English childhood. Therefore one is reluctant to apply to Mr Hudson's book those terms of praise which are bestowed upon literary and artistic merit, though needless to say it possesses both. One does not want to recommend it as a book so much as to greet it as a person, and not the clipped and imperfect person of ordinary autobiography, but the whole and complete person whom we meet rarely enough in life or in literature.

But Mr Hudson himself provides one clue to the secret which we have clumsily tried to prise open. He has been saying that it is difficult not "to retouch, and colour, and shade, and falsify" the picture of childhood by the light of what we have since become. Serge Aksakoff, he goes on to say, in his *History of My Childhood*, was an exception "simply because the temper and tastes and passions of his early boyhood—his intense love of his mother, of nature, of all wild-- ness, and of sport—endured unchanged in him to the end and kept him a boy in heart, able after long years to revive the past mentally and picture it in its true, fresh, and origi- nal colours". That is true also of Mr Hudson. When he writes of himself as a little boy he does not get out of his large body into a small different one, or fall into that vein of half humorous and romantic reverie which the recollection of our small predecessor usually inspires. The little boy whom he remembers was already set with even fresher passion upon the same objects that Mr Hudson has sought all his life. Therefore he has not to reconstruct himself, but only to intensify. It seems, too, as if it must be the easiest thing in the world to remember clearly such a childhood as his was, spent not in some cranny, artificially scooped out of the grown-up world, but in a place naturally fitted and arranged for it. His father lived in a vast house on "the illimitable grassy plain of South America", at a little dis- tance from a plantation of various kinds of trees which were the nesting-place of many different birds. A man upon horseback raised three or four feet above the surrounding level would see all round

> a flat land, its horizon a perfect ring of misty blue colour, where the crystal blue dome of the sky rests on the level green world.... On all this visible world there were no fences and no trees excepting those which had been planted at the old estancia houses, and these being far apart the groves and plantations looked like small islands of trees, or mounds, blue in the distance, on the great plain or pampa.... The picture that most often presents itself is of the cattle coming home in the evening; the green quiet plain extending away from the gate to the horizon; the western sky flushed with sunset hues, and the herd of four or five hundred cattle trotting homewards with loud lowings and bellowings, raising a great cloud of dust with their hoofs, while behind gallop the herdsmen urging them on with wild cries.

One is inclined to hold the view, indeed, that parents of children have no business to live anywhere except on the pampas of South America. For beyond the daily ecstasy of living out of doors, fate seems to have seen to it that the few human beings who wandered into the large house as guests, beggars or tutors summed up in their persons the most marked characteristics of humanity. There was Captain Scott, captain of what is unknown, but an Englishman of immense bulk, "with a great round face of a purplish red colour", dressed always in a light blue suit, who would arrive with his pockets bulging with sweets from the distant land where sweets were made, and stand, "looking like a vast blue pillar", motionless upon the bank, rod in hand. Unknown in origin, he disappeared to an unknown fate, "yet in my mind how beautiful his gigantic image looks!" Then every seven or eight weeks the Hermit arrived, to beg not money but food, which he would take only in the form of flawless biscuits, for should they be chipped or cracked he would have none of them. He was supposed to have committed some terrible crime, which he expiated by wearing a very thick mattress stuffed with sticks, stones, lumps of clay, horns, and other heavy objects, enough to weigh down two men, which he dragged about with him, in penance for what no one knew, since he could speak no intelligible language and died under his mattress alone on the plains without confessing the nature of his crime. The supply of tutors in the pampas was also limited to men who had mysterious reasons of their own, whether it was a devotion to white Brazilian rum or difficulties with the Roman Catholic Church, for choosing a nomadic life and being unable to retain their employment for long. Mr Trigg, for example, "followed teaching because all work was excessively irksome to him", and was hired by the month, like the shepherd or the cowman, to teach children their letters, until his failing found him out, and, in spite of his delightful social gifts and his passion for reading Dickens aloud, he had to take to his horse again and ride off with a bag containing all his possessions over the plains.

With reluctance one must resist the temptation of transcribing one such character sketch after another, not only because the transcription damages the pleasure of coming upon the page itself, but also because to give the impression that the book is mainly composed of such sketches would not be true. The remarkably handsome young gentleman with a wash-leather bag attached to his wrist who threw pebbles at small birds on the Parade at Buenos Aires, the immensely fat lady who sat perpetually on a cane chair attended by four hairless dogs, the three on the floor "ever patiently waiting for their respective turns to occupy the broad warm lap", the stranger who played divinely on the guitar but could not go on playing for thinking of his own family in Spain, Don Gregorio with his passion for breeding piebald horses and his rage against anyone possessed of such an animal who refused to sell it—all these figures met the eyes of the observant little boy, and are faithfully presented as the sort of thing that you saw if you looked up in South America from the absorbing business of life. For he was a child, almost a baby, when he discovered instinctively what was the business, or rather the spirit, of life, the string upon which all sights and thoughts and adventures were hereafter to be threaded. He begins as a small child who notices things in the bulk to gaze at the trees in the plantation. It was a "wonderful experience to be among them, to feel and smell their rough, moist, bark, stained green with moss, and to look up at the blue sky through the network of interlacing twigs". Then those trees became full of birds, and Mr Hudson is constantly tempted to make "this sketch of my first years a book about birds and little else". He resists the temptation, but, like all writers of strong individuality, a colour gets into his pages apart from the actual words, and even when they are not mentioned we seem to see the bird flying, settling, feeding, soaring through every page of the book. There are the immensely tall white-and-rose-coloured birds of earliest memory who stand feeding in the river and then shake out their wings, which are of a glorious crimson colour; then the resounding screams of the travelling parrots are heard, and they appear, flying at a moderate height, "with long pointed wings and long graduated tails, in their sombre green plumage touched with yellow, blue, and crimson colour". These are the birds of earliest childhood, and from them his dreams spring and by them his images are coloured in later life. Riding at first seemed to him like flying. When he is first among a crowd of well-dressed people in Buenos Aires he compares them at once to a flock of military starlings. From watching birds comes his lifelong desire to fly—but it is a desire which no airship or balloon but the wings of a bird alone will satisfy. Later these first impressions were intensified by his habit of rambling off alone and standing motionless, staring at vacancy as his mother, following him in anxiety for his state of mind, supposed; but to her joy she found that he was not staring at vacancy, but observing "an insect perhaps, but oftener a bird".

And yet if we were to say that on this account Mr Hudson's book is written chiefly for naturalists it would not be true. The naturalist will see the bird accurately enough, but he will not see it in relation to the tree, to the small boy, to the strange characters of the plain; nor will the bodies of birds represent for him that mysterious spirit which Mr Hudson, for some reason that psychologists must explain, finds in all nature, but in birds particularly. Because Mr Hudson is able to do all this, to read his book is to read another chapter in that enormous book which is written from time to time by Rousseau and Borrow and George Sand and Aksakoff among other people—a book which we can never read enough of; and therefore we must beg Mr Hudson not to stop here, but to carry the story on to the farthest possible limits.

Honest Fiction

Review of *Shops and Houses*, by Frank Swinnerton.
(10 October, 1918.)

SHOPS AND HOUSES is one of those books which by their health and robustness should confute those who hold that English fiction is in a languid or degenerate condition. There can be no reason for despondency or for disparaging comparisons when novels of such care and conscience and ability are produced, not of course in any quantity, but still by a small and undaunted band of writers, among whom we must now place Mr Swinnerton. He is among the group of honest observers of contemporary life who filter their impressions sedulously and uncompromisingly through the intellect and suffer nothing to pass save what possesses meaning and solidity.

It is not necessary that Mr Swinnerton should say anything very strange or very unpleasant in *Shops and Houses*. He sets out to show us the life in a suburb not far from London where the men work in the city all day and the women spend their time ordering their households, going to tea parties, and buying things in shops. Mr Swinnerton takes up his position upon a little mound of intellectual honesty, from which he observes and according to which he judges. Perhaps there once happened to him what happened to his hero Louis Vechantor at the Hughes's tea party. ". . . He seemed for a moment to lose consciousness. The tea-table chatter sounded like the confused roaring of a crowd some distance away. . . . Their laughter seemed to him like the grinning of skulls. . . . Louis had never fainted, or he would have known that a curious sweet remoteness precedes the total loss of sensation. It was just that feeling of being apart and contemplative that had assailed him." *Shops and Houses* may well have had its origin in some such moment of remoteness at a tea party, but, having seen his vision, Mr Swinnerton set to work to search out and verify every detail that went to compose the large effect; and as each was received it was tested by a standard which we may roughly describe as the standard of intellectual honesty. How did they live, what did they live for, what were these healthy unemployed young women, these indolent elderly ladies, after? He has discovered an astonishing number of very minute facts as to the manner in which the ladies of Beckwith perform their chief occupation in life—the "consumption of precious time". He is with them when they wish to attract, and when they cease to wish to attract; he observes their attempts to marry or to prevent marriage; he sees them piecing together into interminable romances little shreds of gossip picked from the dust-heap. He examines the process by which the public opinion of Beckwith is formed, and traces it in operation upon a case specially submitted to it. How would Beckwith, he asks, deal with the case of a respectable resident's disreputable cousin who has the effrontery to set up a grocer's shop in Beckwith itself? By means of details and fragments he has set working a model Beckwith which performs all the functions of spending time with the regularity of an ant-heap; or, since the activity of an ant-heap has some direction, with the automatic accuracy of a decapitated duck. Moreover, he has created what he dissects. He is not only the "disembodied and cruel spectator"; he has enough sympathy to show us, at any rate through the eyes of Louis Vechantor, that there were possibilities and varieties among the people of Beckwith which make them momentarily attractive and intermittently pathetic.

But although there are passages of hope, Beckwith does not pass the test; Beckwith is shown up; as Dorothy Vechantor, who is appointed to wind up the spiritual affairs of Beckwith, says, "I've been thinking whether perhaps Beckwith . . . that it isn't altogether a place at all. I mean whether it isn't a sort of disease." In saying this she lays her finger not only upon the deficiency of Beckwith, but upon the deficiency which *Shops and Houses* shares with so many other novels of the intellectual school. Beckwith is proved to be a disease: it has failed to pass any of the tests which Mr Swinnerton so honestly and acutely applies; it is snobbish and vulgar, cruel, stupid, without worth, rhyme, or reason. Nevertheless, with all these proofs of its spiritual bankruptcy before us, we still remain unconvinced. Our lack of

conviction is not, as at first sight appears, because of the
incredible meanness and insignificance of the crimes cited
against the inhabitants, although their minuteness certainly
diminishes their power to affect us; we cannot believe that
Beckwith is merely a disease because we cannot accept Mr
Swinnerton's view of what constitutes health. Louis
Vechantor and Dorothy, the daughter of the grocer, the
grocer William, and the grocer's family are the represen-
tatives of sincerity and humanity. They are capable of
thought and capable of love. They are the martyrs whom
Beckwith half succeeds in pelting to death with its grains of
spite; it is to them that we look with confidence to champion
the human cause. And it is precisely these characters who
fail us. Those scenes which should show us the honesty and
energy of life removed from the burden of false convention
are the weakest in the book. It is by their failure that we are
led to doubt whether honesty and intelligence will really
do all that the intellectual novelist claims for them, and
whether because of their absence we are entitled to blot a
whole suburb from the map. Perhaps there are other
qualities, other aims, other desires which make even Miss
Lampe of Station Road a little more complex than an
agitated ant or a decapitated duck? Perhaps there is more
in marriage, love, friendship, beauty than Mr Swinnerton
altogether conveys? But, we repeat, it is a great thing that
Beckwith should be destroyed; it is a most valuable work.

September

Review of *September*, by Frank Swinnerton.
(25 September, 1919.)

SEPTEMBER is a better book than *Shops and Houses*. It is, indeed, a very able book. With candour and with sincerity Mr Swinnerton has applied his brain to a very difficult task. Here is a woman, Marian Forster by name, aged thirty-eight, no longer in love with her husband, but affectionate and tolerant of his occasional lapses. By no means for the first time she discovers that he is in love, but this time it is with a friend of hers, Cherry Mant, a girl of twenty-two. She takes her husband's conduct very much for granted; it is the question of the girl that puzzles her. What is her intention? How far is she culpable? What is the relation between them as hostess and guest, mature woman and undeveloped girl, living for the time in the same country house? Later, Nigel Sinclair, a young man nearer Cherry's age than her own, makes his appearance. He falls in love with Mrs Forster, she with him, yet at the critical moment she stops short. She cannot give herself away; something checks her, and the moment passes. Still in love with him as she is, she realizes the presence of an obstacle, undefined at first, later revealed, and once more discovered to be the same girl, Cherry Mant. Believing that his rejection was final, Nigel Sinclair had gone to her and fallen in love with her. But Nigel Sinclair scarcely counts. The relationship between the two women is the theme of the book; and as Mr Swinnerton has been at pains to endow each with character, and to make out from his own insight how such a relation might shape itself, the development is original enough to have an unusual air of truth.

Given a woman close on forty, naturally reserved, intelligent enough to be detached, with an obstinate conviction of the importance of conduct, neither love nor jealousy has free play. She will always be taking them up and passing them before the light of other ideals.

It was insight that Marian craved. She incessantly sought

it. She may have been a dull woman, a woman remote from the pursuit of ordinary pleasures; but at least she had this single ideal. . . . She desired nothing but the improvement of the world. She could accept nothing less than the disinterested pursuit of clear and noble ends.

From this standpoint "the clear and noble" thing to be aimed at is not, in the present case, personal happiness. Neither is it the luxury of denunciation. Mrs Forster in pursuing her ideals has to bring about the union of the man she loves with her rival. She has also so to scrutinize her feelings that affection predominates over jealousy in her relations with Cherry Mant. Her own spoils from the contest are neither romantic nor showy, and the conclusion is of an autumnal quality. She achieves nothing for herself but courage and the power to sympathize with others; and Mr Swinnerton caps his work with the sentence that "if it is not the first of gifts, it is among those most rarely bestowed upon poor mortals, and is without price".

Mrs Forster's figure is finely and logically outlined, because the intellect has had much to do with the shaping of it; and wherever Mr Swinnerton can use his brain he uses it to good effect. But the figure of Cherry Mant is a much more hazardous piece of work Ideals have no such consistent control over her. The intellect is there, but it is at the mercy of a thousand instincts. Once more we are reminded of the supreme difficulty of transferring the mind of one sex into that of the other. The mental changes which each woman produces in the other are credible for the most part, always interesting and often subtle. Yet it is impossible not to hear, as the close tense narrative proceeds, a sound as of the cutting of steps in ice. Mr Swinnerton is making a little too sure because at heart he is not sure at all. Up we go; firmly we plant our feet, but not without a sense of effort; the atmosphere is dry; the scene a little bare. It is easy enough to mark out the boundaries of Mr Swinnerton's talent—to say that his is a lucid rather than a beautiful mind, intellectual in its scope, rather than imaginative. But praise ought to have the last word and the weightiest. For among modern novelists very few would choose to make the fruit of the contest something so quiet and, until we give it a second look, so ordinary as the power which Marian Forster retrieved from the wreck of brighter hopes. Few would plan their story so consistently with that end in view. We read with the conviction that we are being asked to attend to a problem worth solving—a conviction so rare as by itself to prove that *September* is a novel of exceptional merit.

The Three Black Pennys

Review of *The Three Black Pennies*, by Joseph Hergesheimer.
(12 December, 1918.)

THE obvious thing to say about Mr Joseph Hergesheimer's novel *The Three Black Pennys* is that it possesses
form as undoubtedly as a precious stone shaped to fit exactly
into a band of gold possesses form. The comparison with
something hard, lustrous and concrete is not altogether
fanciful. In recollection, the last sentence being read, the
reader's impression of the book as a whole assumes something of the smooth solidity of a well-fashioned gem. When
the last sentence is finished nothing vague or superfluous is
left to blur the outline; the substance is all neatly packed
into the form, rounded off, disposed of, completed. The
sense of conclusiveness is so satisfactory, and also so rare,
that we could enjoy it separately from any feeling of pity or
pleasure aroused by the fortunes of the characters, as a
blind man might enjoy the shape of a stone though unable
to see its colour.

Mr Hergesheimer's story, the story of a family owning a
great ironworks in Pennsylvania from the middle of the
eighteenth century to modern times, had need of this
shaping if only to compress it within a volume of moderate
size. Each of the Pennys whom he has selected to represent
his theme stands out from the rest of his family because the
Welsh blood mixed with the English blood centuries ago
asserts itself in him. It produces, Howat's father says, "a
solitary living, dark lot. Unamenable to influence, reflect
their country, I suppose, but lovers of music . . . it sinks
entirely out of sight for two or three and sometimes four
generations; and then appears solid, in one individual, as
unslacked as the pure, original thing." It appears in
Howat; in his grandson Jasper; in Jasper's grandson Howat,
the last of the Pennys. The black Pennys did not take to life
easily; there was something unmalleable in their composition which stayed unmelted in the common furnace.
They did not run into the ordinary social mould. In their

obdurate ways of impressing themselves upon other people they more resembled the great hammer at Myrtle Forge, persistently and relentlessly beating out iron, than the iron itself. "If the hammer stops," Howat told his wife in the eighteenth century, "all this, the Pennys, stop, too." The last Penny was unable even to make one of those marriages which his ancestors had achieved with so much difficulty; the hammer had stopped in his father's time; the Pennys made iron no longer.

But the story cannot, as this summary might suggest, be read as a discourse upon heredity with a satiric motive; Mr Hergesheimer is too much of an artist to insist that human life is capable of any such forced solution. If, curiously enough, a certain type of character occurs at intervals in the same family, it occurs as a blue or a green might repeat itself beautifully in a pattern. The beat of the great hammer recurs too; when it stops we know that something more important has ceased; the raccoon hunt repeats itself; for, as we began by saying, Mr Hergesheimer has a strong sense of form, and these are some of the more obvious devices used by him to hold his story together, to secure continuity, to bind his gem in a circle of gold. An attentive reader will discover others less obvious. Whether he has succeeded equally in another direction is more open to doubt. The entrances and exits of the Pennys and of the women allotted them as partners are so carefully timed and regulated that they would tend to be mechanical were they not more obviously pictorial. There is no room here for license or for the larger sweep and expressiveness of human character. Perhaps Mr Hergesheimer is a little hampered in this direction by his keen susceptibility to material objects. He handles, for the concrete term is justified, his blue decanters and cut-glass decanters, holds them to the light, relishes their grain and texture with a gusto which is sometimes excessive. He cannot resist observing. We can remember no novel in which women's dresses are more frequently and carefully described. This is not done, however, to give atmosphere or local colour, but because the beauty of still life makes part of the writer's vision. We owe to this indi-vidual gift some remarkable scenes at the forge and descriptions of American landscape. It is one of the qualities that make the Black Pennys an unusual novel, to be read slowly, thoughtfully and with a sense of luxury.

Java Head

Review of *Java Head*, by Joseph Hergesheimer.
(29 May, 1919.)

THE THREE BLACK PENNYS was a very good
novel; *Java Head* is a good novel. But, even so, *Java
Head* is quite good enough to deserve that we should bring
forward our reasons for judging it decidedly inferior to its
predecessor. Every writer, after the first flush of youthful
experiment, settles into a manner of his own. It is inevitable;
and yet, as the new scene shapes itself after the pattern of the
old, as the sentence takes its accustomed curve, some little
thrill of foreboding may stay the pen in the air. These easy
cadences and facile arrangements are the first grey hairs,
the first intimations of senility. There is only one way to
remain young: it is to cease doing what you have learnt to do
easily and perhaps successfully, and to attempt what you
are not certain of being able to do at all. The odious discip-
line which we should prescribe for Mr Hergesheimer is to
write a novel in which there is no furniture, no ladies'
dresses, no still life. He should be forced to write of modern
people; he should be required to make them talk. For the
comparative failure of *Java Head* is due to a self-indulgence
which eliminates all that Mr Hergesheimer finds difficult
or repellent and leaves those problems which he enjoys
solving and is certain of solving exquisitely as often as he
chooses.

Again we have America some hundred years ago. The
scene is laid at Salem. The family of Ammidon, with whom
the story is chiefly concerned, is a great shipowning family.
They trade with the East, and the beautiful sailing ships
laden with picturesque cargoes furl their sails almost under
the windows of the substantial dwelling-house which the
old sea captain, Jeremy Ammidon, has christened Java
Head, after the high black rock which was "the symbol of
the safe and happy end of an arduous voyage". One day his
son, the sea captain Gerrit, after being given up for lost, sails
into the harbour, and along with his casks and bales brings
to shore an unknown bride, a Chinese woman of the highest

caste. Exposed to the chatter and gossip of Salem society, Taou Yuen remains imperturbable and alien. The love-making of Edward Dunsack, a merchant trading with China, acquainted with the language and demoralized by the smoking of opium, scarcely rouses her. But through him she learns to suspect her husband's fidelity. He was, she is told, in love with Dunsack's niece. During her visit to the suspected girl Dunsack breaks into the room, and to escape the horrors pressing round her Taou Yuen snatches his opium pills, swallows one after another, and dies in her sleep.

But as in a picture the eye rests on some tuft of daisies or spray of foliage while conscious of the larger lines, so these details are part of the surrounding landscape. At the same time that Taou Yuen loves and dies, the old sea captain Jeremy faces the fact that the slow-sailing ships of his youth and pride are outdone by the new racing clippers, and dies of the shock of finding that without his knowledge two of the company's vessels are engaged in the opium trade. Somehow, too, it is not merely jealousy that has killed the Chinese woman, but America, with its "unfamiliar circumstances, tradition, emotions". The presence of a scaffolding of this sort gives *Java Head* its sobriety and distinction. And, to continue a metaphor which is peculiarly suitable to Mr Hergesheimer, the painting of the little tufts and sprigs is at once loving and precise. Take this, for instance, of the Nautilus coming into harbour: "The ship moved more slowly, under her topsails and jibs, in a soundless progress with the ripples falling away in water like dark green glass, liquid and still." Or take one of the many descriptions of the apparel of Taou Yuen. She wore

a long gown with wide sleeves of blue-black satin, embroidered in peach-coloured flower petals and innumerable minute sapphire and orange butterflies, a short sleeveless jacket of sage green caught with looped red jade buttons and threaded with silver, and indigo high-soled slippers crusted and tasselled with pearls. Her hair rose from the back in a smooth burnished loop. There were long pins of pink jade carved into blossoms, a quivering decoration of paper-thin gold leaves

with moonstones in glistening drops, and a band of coral lotus
buds. Pierced stone bracelets—

but it is too long to quote in its entirety; worse, it is too
detailed to be seen as a whole. Happily Mr Hergesheimer
has himself saved us from uttering the priggish comment
which keeps breaking in among these pretty things. "She is
very gorgeous and placid, superior on the surface; but the
heart, Gerrit—that isn't made of jade and ivory and silk."
No, the heart is neither gorgeous nor placid. It is very
difficult to write beautifully about the heart. When Mr
Hergesheimer has to describe not what people wear but
what they feel, he shows his lack of ease or of interest by
becoming either very violent or very stiff. There is no sense
of enjoyment in his dialogue.

The origin of this fault-finding, however, is to be found
in the fact that *Java Head* is one of the smaller number of
novels which appear to be written by an adult; and therefore we make Mr Hergesheimer responsible for our disappointment instead of saying nothing about it, because it is
useless to point out the immaturity of a child. He brings to
mind some of the novelists who are undoubtedly immature
—Mr Conrad, for example. And one of their peculiarities
is that felicities of the kind we have quoted come incidentally on the search for something higher and more rewarding
so that we take them in half consciously at the time as part
of the general richness, and only in memory go back and
distinguish them for their individual beauty. But in *Java
Head* we are led up to them; they are the fruit on the top-
most branch; there is nothing beyond them. Nevertheless,
Java Head is a good novel.

Gold and Iron

Review of *Gold and Iron*, by Joseph Hergesheimer.
(25 December, 1919.)

IN developing a photograph first one black patch appears
on the greyish film and then another. By degrees the
square of the picture defines itself; here is the edge of a
wall; here, isolated but unmistakable, the outline of a
croquet hoop. One rocks the fluid from side to side, and
watches anxiously for an increasing thickening and intric-
acy, or the film will certainly prove either under exposed or
over. Thus with the books of Mr Joseph Hergesheimer, now
appearing with such frequency, one watches anxiously to
see whether the undoubted eminence of his talent in this
respect and that will be supported all round by other gifts
until the picture covers the whole surface of the film and we
are in possession of a complete work of art.

"Wild Oranges", the first story in the present book, *Gold
and Iron*, suggests that Mr Hergesheimer is still in process of
development. There is no doubt at all that he is mature in
certain respects. He wants to describe a ship, a shore, a
deserted house, an orange tree, and he does it directly,
succinctly, with the assurance of maturity. He gets the
essential background with little effort and considerable
mastery. But, remembering *Java Head*, it is with some
anxiety that we see a woman's shape emerging upon the
film. For women will talk, and that is where Mr Hergesheimer hitherto has come to grief. Millie Stopes, who has
been marooned on the coast of Georgia in company with a
homicidal lunatic and a father who fled from Virginia forty
years ago because in the Civil War women hung an apron
on his door, has every reason to be, like the wild oranges that
grew round the house, thick of rind and bitter of flavour.
But set her, as she stoops catching fish in her solitude, by the
side of some girl in Mr Conrad's pages, and you feel that
here Mr Hergesheimer's talent ebbs and deserts him. She
is a silhouette posed a trifle melodramatically against the
sunset; and, as usual, the sunset is more vivid than the
woman. There is something set and sterile about her. But

just as we are making this point another speck on the film catches our eyes and, developing, changes the picture once more: John Woolfolk, the sailor who has dropped anchor opposite the ruined house, takes Millie for a sail. She is terrified by the open sea. He has to put back to shore again. The yacht anchors in the bay and Millie sits brooding on the deck. "What is it," she demanded of John Woolfolk, "that lives in our own hearts and betrays our utmost convictions and efforts, and destroys us against all knowledge and desire?" "It may be called heredity," he replied. That perhaps derives from Ibsen, but at any rate we feel a new force blowing through the stiff, still pages. Mr Hergesheimer makes for the open sea with a theme behind him.

The two stories that follow are better composed, but not so interesting as the first. For one thing Mr Hergesheimer goes back to his iron masters and his seaport life of a hundred years ago; and, though the stories display his good qualities, they seem, to recur to the photographic figure, to be arrested in their development. In the act of asserting their passion his figures are stricken with frost; and yet the gesture is always a fine one. Our conclusion, then, must be—but happily we do not feel impelled to come to a conclusion. "Wild Oranges" justifies us in holding our judgment in suspense. Mr Hergesheimer is still in process of development.

The Pursuit of Beauty

Review of *Linda Condon*, by Joseph Hergesheimer. (8 July, 1920.)

AMONG the advantages of having been born three or four centuries ago one cannot help including, perhaps wrongly, the advantage of having no past. The consciousness then was not impeded at every point by the knowledge of what had been said in that book, or painted on that canvas. In particular, writers like Mr Hergesheimer, whose sense of beauty is exceptionally lusty, would have gratified it more simply and fully than is likely to be possible again. Writing now with beauty as one's theme, how can one avoid taking as symbols of two different ideals two statues, both of extreme antiquity, one the grayish-green image of a squat Chinese god, the other the white figure of the Greek Victory? One would wish to avoid it, because symbols are, unfortunately, apt to impose themselves. Linda Condon and Dodge Pleydon both show signs of the mould. They would not have taken this shape, one feels, unless their maker had been deeply versed in book learning. But then, again, it is largely because Mr Hergesheimer is a sophisticated writer that he is an interesting writer. Let us never discourage the novelist from finding strange elements in the composition of modern life. And after all, though Queen Elizabeth was a model of vigour she was also a dirty old woman, dabbling her fingers in the gravy, and amenable, one supposes, to pains and pleasures only of the most direct kind.

The first years of Linda Condon's life were presided over by the green Chinese image with the expression of placid and sneering lust. Stella Condon, her mother, had long lived upon the benefactions of anonymous gentlemen in hotels—a sumptuous life, stuffed with eating and drinking and finery and debauchery. Mr Hergesheimer has no prudery about ugliness. It is the complement of his love of beauty. Plush bedrooms, cosmetics, strewn toilet tables and tumbled underlinen, all that makes the iridescence of decay, is truthfully rendered. More remarkable is his success in making us feel that Stella Condon was alive, even sensitive and warm-hearted, in the midst of the garbage. "Always remember mamma telling you that the most expensive corsets are the cheapest in the end." Such was her life's philosophy, delivered in rather a thick voice, for she was "mussed" with drink, to her daughter of ten. But, nevertheless, she is the most sympathetic and most imaginative figure in the book. Linda, the daughter of this mother and of a vanished father, the son of old tradition and culture, is, rightly no doubt, denied the directness of her mother's appeal. She is anything but direct. Considering the variety and strangeness of the qualities that have been shredded into her, it would have been a rare triumph had she glowed with life.

But life, in the usual sense, is the quality purposely denied her, for is she not, mysteriously, beauty rather than life, the spirit rather than the body, at every turn inhibited from the common responses of the usual woman? It is her function to live in the statue and not in the children of her body. Her soul is preserved by the sculptor, Dodge Pleydon, in bronze, for it is through the man that she exists. When, in a belated attempt to feel the ordinary passions of humanity, she comes to live with him she realizes that it is not her in the flesh but her in the spirit that he desires. Therefore she leaves him to cherish the beautiful body which, at any rate in the expression that he has given to it, is ultimately enough for her, too.

The story lends itself to fantastic treatment, for the freedom of which we find ourselves occasionally hungering. But Mr Hergesheimer keeps to the solid and the actual. The difficult experiment is hardly successful, though the failure is more marked in Dodge Pleydon than in Linda herself. One would have guessed him, were it not for the name on the title page, a woman's hero—large, brutal, brilliant, cherishing in a lacquer box a lost glove. The icy finger of theory has chilled him, so that one feels him not fantastic but unreal. That charge might be levelled against Linda herself also, but in a different sense. She is like one of those watches that are made too elaborately to be able to go. Yet, though we hold it the supreme merit of watches to be able to go, as Stella Condon goes, there is great pleasure to be had in these delicate mechanisms. They are well worth picking to pieces.

Pleasant Stories

Review of *The Happy End*, by Joseph Hergesheimer.
(16 December, 1920.)

W
HEN Mr Hergesheimer says, "These stories have but
one purpose—to give pleasure," every reviewer will
wish himself a novelist. It is more blessed, that is to say, to
give simply and freely than to receive cautiously and ques-
tioningly. Of course Mr Hergesheimer gives us pleasure,
but so do bright fires, oysters, and clean sheets. It is the dis-
mal office of the reviewer to splinter pleasure into separate
pieces which he examines, compares, and judges to be good,
better, or best. Excitement, for example—is that the right
kind of pleasure or the wrong? About two pages before the
end of each of Mr Hergesheimer's seven stories the hand
slips out and lies across the print in order to bar the eye
from leaping and galloping to the end. Reviewers are epi-
cures. If we read too quick we know that we shall miss the
niceties of this careful, economical, and well-trained crafts-
man. "Below, the water was invisible in the wrap of night.
Naples shone like a pale gold net drawn about the sweep of
its hills. A glow like a thumb-print hung over Vesuvius;
the hidden column of smoke smudged the stars." The wrap,
the net, the thumb-print smudging the stars will each, if
you spare the time, yield a little drop of pleasure. Mr
Hergesheimer's pages are always strewn with such felicities.
He has a fine sense of matter. Still, even the great masters of
material description, as Keats was in "The Eve of St
Agnes," always seem to be doing the easy thing when they
are doing that. Must we suspect that our pleasure in the
"gowns by Verlat" and the pink pearl necklace is a little
gross and indolent? That is putting it too harshly. For, as
we say, we have to read on. The stories are far too well
contrived to smother us in old lace or hypnotize us with
pink pearls while down below the bullfighter is challenging
the banker to a duel. Indeed, the main source of our pleasure is that so many things happen and happen so quickly,
and seem to be happening to such solid people. For though
the space is small and the movements to be gone through in

that space many and violent, Mr Hergesheimer gives his figures considerable body. They are forcibly cut out with strong, clean strokes. Perhaps the heaviest meal we have ever eaten in fiction occurs in "Bread". As we sit munching solidly through the courses with August Turnbull, we begin to feel that our pleasure is really respectable. The clams, the turtle soup, the thick crimson slices of beef, the ice, the coffee, the long dark roll of oily tobacco, are the right symbols for the man and his life. He will not escape his fate, and his fate will be fitting and satisfactory; and we shall feel that we have been let into a secret about life, which is perhaps the most pleasurable sensation there is. Judge, then, of our disappointment when a melodramatic boat drifts, as if towed invisibly by a cinema man in a tug, ashore at Turnbull's feet, containing a crew of starved, lead-coloured corpses on top of whom Turnbull of course falls dead, solely, as we feel, to give us an extra dollop of pleasure.

In short, if you look back over these seven stories, you will find that your pleasure has come from things that happen and not from the people to whom they happen. Adequate and lifelike as they are, they are obedient dolls to be disposed of, and will fold their limbs and fit into the box when the play is over. We say this with regret, because many of them have acted their parts vigorously and well. Mr Hergesheimer might rightly urge that, if he had let them dawdle about and get ideas into their heads, nothing would have happened. No box would have held them. Very likely we should have been bored. And are we sure that we should not have sacrificed a certain pleasure for one that is not merely uncertain, but also extremely mixed, compounded of all sorts of sighs, hints, hesitations, nebulous and yet startling, full of horror and illumination? Why think of Tchehov when one is reading Mr Hergesheimer? Why spoil what we have by imagining what we have not? Only because it is, in our opinion, a good thing to take writers seriously; for then perhaps they will think it worth their while to give us not simply pleasure, but a good kind of pleasure—for which our appetite is unbounded.

Mummery

Review of *Mummery*, by G. Cannan. (19 December, 1918.)

MUMMERY, which is apparently the nineteenth volume from Mr Cannan's pen, is a clever readable novel, as we have some reason to expect that an author's nineteenth book should be. Nineteen volumes cannot be brought from start to finish without learning whatever you are capable of learning about writing books; but the risk of learning your lesson so thoroughly is that you may become in the process not an artist, but a professional writer. You may learn to write so easily that writing becomes a habit. Mr Cannan has to tell the story of two men of genius, one a painter, the other a dramatist; both would reform the stage, one by his designs, the other by his plays; but they are both frustrated, so far as the present is concerned, by the British public and by Sir Henry Butcher, the actor-manager, who serves that public faithfully or with only an occasional disloyalty. The theatrical world is very vivaciously and very literally represented by Mr Cannan, so that many of the characters in it seem to belong as much to the actual world as to the world of fiction. But whether or not he has his counterpart in life, Sir Henry Butcher is certainly the most imaginative character in the book. One can believe that actor-managers famed for their sumptuous representations of Shakespeare, as illustrious in society as upon the stage, in whom strangely enough the dramatic genius burns up by fits and starts, are much as Mr Cannan depicts them. The wealthy peer who supports the higher drama, the manager's wife who regards the theatre "as a kind of salon" and hates any attempt "to divert Sir Henry from the social to the professional aspect of the theatre", the atmosphere of the Imperium behind the scenes and in the boxes, are all done skilfully and with humour.

So long as Mr Cannan is noting down what he has observed he shows himself a shrewd though not a very subtle observer. But when he draws conclusions from what he has seen and becomes the intellectual satirist, he writes as if from habit, repeating what he has learnt by heart from writers of what he calls "the Sturm and Drang period" in whom the intellect was often very keen and the satiric gift very fine. Mr Adnor Rodd is their representative. The name is sufficient to show us that, let alone the distinguished appearance and the abrupt manner. But Mr Adnor Rodd, though he is a very conscientious man and writes plays which no one will produce, is not, so far as our experience goes, a very clever man. "Money!" he exclaims. "That is the secret of the whole criminal business. Money controls art. Money rejects art. Money's a sensitive thing too. It rejects force, spontaneity, originality. It wants repetition, immutability, things calculable. Money..." He is, in short, what the conventional idea of an artist is supposed to be, "demoniac and challenging"; just as Charles Mann, the painter, is the irresponsible and non-moral variety of the same type. Sir Henry Butcher and the Imperium theatre are quite proof against attacks levelled at them by people of this calibre, and deserve to be so. But it is a misfortune from the point of view of the book, in so far as it is a book of criticism and ideas. Mr Cannan has every right to criticize society in his books, but, like everything else in a novel criticism must be the expression of a writer's own convictions; the conventions of the intellectual are at least as sterile as the conventions of the bourgeois. Mr Cannan seems to be falling into the habit of being intellectual in a perfectly conventional way, so that his criticism is more and more a stereotyped complaint and his remedy more and more a nostrum made up for him by other people. If he had thought out his position afresh and for himself, he would scarcely have spoilt Clara Day by making her half a natural nice woman and half the embodiment of somebody's theory upon the function of the female sex in human society. "Her childish detestation of her womanhood was gone. She accepted it, gloried in it as her instrument, and knew that she could never be lost in it. For ever in her mind that crisis was associated with Kropotkin's escape from prison." On the advice, no doubt, of some distinguished writer, she saw "that being a woman, she must work through a man's imagination before she could become a person fit to dwell on the earth with her fellows", and married Rodd; but a marriage so cordially vouched for by the best authorities has no need of our commendation. It is in Mr Cannan's interest, and not in Mr and Mrs Rodd's, that we recommend him to find some means of destroying the careful selection of books, including six volumes of Ibsen, which they took with them on their honeymoon.

The Tunnel

Review of *The Tunnel*, by Dorothy Richardson.
(13 February, 1919.)

ALTHOUGH *The Tunnel* is the fourth book that Miss
Richardson has written, she must still expect to find
her reviewers paying a great deal of attention to her method.
It is a method that demands attention, as a door whose
handle we wrench ineffectively calls our attention to the
fact that it is locked. There is no slipping smoothly down
the accustomed channels; the first chapters provide an
amusing spectacle of hasty critics seeking them in vain. If
this were the result of perversity, we should think Miss
Richardson more courageous than wise; but being, as we
believe, not wilful but natural, it represents a genuine
conviction of the discrepancy between what she has to say
and the form provided by tradition for her to say it in. She
is one of the rare novelists who believe that the novel is so
much alive that it actually grows. As she makes her advanced critic, Mr Wilson, remark: "There will be books with
all that cut out—him and her—all that sort of thing. The
book of the future will be clear of all that." And Miriam
Henderson herself reflects: "but if books were written like
that, sitting down and doing it cleverly and knowing just
what you were doing and just how somebody else had done
it, there was something wrong, some mannish cleverness
that was only half right. To write books knowing all about
style would be to become like a man." So "him and her" are
cut out, and with them goes the old deliberate business: the
chapters that lead up and the chapters that lead down;
the characters who are always characteristic; the scenes
that are passionate and the scenes that are humorous; the
elaborate construction of reality; the conception that shapes
and surrounds the whole. All these things are cast away, and
there is left, denuded, unsheltered, unbegun and unfinished,
the consciousness of Miriam Henderson, the small sensitive
lump of matter, half transparent and half opaque, which
endlessly reflects and distorts the variegated procession, and

is, we are bidden to believe, the source beneath the surface, the very oyster within the shell.

The critic is thus absolved from the necessity of picking out the themes of the story. The reader is not provided with a story; he is invited to embed himself in Miriam Henderson's consciousness, to register one after another, and one on top of another, words, cries, shouts, notes of a violin, fragments of lectures, to follow these impressions as they flicker through Miriam's mind, waking incongruously other thoughts, and plaiting incessantly the many-coloured and innumerable threads of life. But a quotation is better than description.

> She was surprised now at her familiarity with the details of the room . . . that idea of visiting places in dreams. It was something more than that . . . all the real part of your life has a real dream in it; some of the real dream part of you coming true. You know in advance when you are really following your life. These things are familiar because reality is here. Coming events cast *light*. It is like dropping everything and walking backward to something you know is there. However far you go out you come back. . . . I am back now where I was before I began trying to do things like other people. I left home to get here. None of those things can touch me here. They are mine.

Here we are thinking, word by word, as Miriam thinks. The method, if triumphant, should make us feel ourselves seated at the centre of another mind, and, according to the artistic gift of the writer, we should perceive in the helter-skelter of flying fragments some unity, significance, or design. That Miss Richardson gets so far as to achieve a sense of reality far greater than that produced by the ordinary means is undoubted. But, then, which reality is it, the superficial or the profound? We have to consider the quality of Miriam Henderson's consciousness, and the extent to which Miss Richardson is able to reveal it. We have to decide whether the flying helter-skelter resolves itself by degrees into a perceptible whole. When we are in a position to make up our minds we cannot deny a slight sense of disappointment. Having sacrificed not merely "hims and hers", but so many seductive graces of wit and style for the prospect of some new revelation or greater intensity, we still find ourselves distressingly near the surface. Things look much the same as ever. It is certainly a very vivid surface. The consciousness of Miriam takes the reflection of a dentist's room to perfection. Her senses of touch, sight and hearing are all excessively acute. But sensations, impressions, ideas and emotions glance off her, unrelated and unquestioned, without shedding quite as much light as we had hoped into the hidden depths. We find ourselves in the dentist's room, in the street, in the lodging-house bedroom frequently and convincingly; but never, or only for a tantalizing second, in the reality which underlies these appearances. In particular, the figures of other people on whom Miriam casts her capricious light are vivid enough, but their sayings and doings never reach that degree of significance which we, perhaps unreasonably, expect. The old method seems sometimes the more profound and economical of the two. But it must be admitted that we are exacting. We want to be rid of realism, to penetrate without its help into the regions beneath it, and further require that Miss Richardson shall fashion this new material into something which has the shapeliness of the old accepted forms. We are asking too much; but the extent of our asking proves that *The Tunnel* is better in its failure than most books in their success.

Romance and the Heart

Review of *The Grand Tour*, by Romer Wilson, and
Revolving Lights, by Dorothy Richardson. (19 May, 1923.)

BOTH Miss Wilson and Miss Richardson are serious
novelists, and we must therefore put our minds at their
service with the consciousness that, though criticize them
we must, something of positive value, which that criticism
should reveal, remains. And in trying to make out what this
gift of theirs amounts to it is not necessary to go with great
detail into the particular examples before us. Each writer is
mature; each has written many books, and here, again, each
is doing her own work in her own way.

Miss Wilson is a romantic. That is the first impression
which her vigour and freedom make upon us. While other
novelists sit studying the skeleton of humanity and painfully
tracing the relations of tiny fibres, Miss Wilson hurls a
sponge at the blackboard, takes her way into the forest,
flings herself on a couch of amaranth, and revels in the
thunder. For her not only the sky, but the soul too, is always
thundering and lightening. There are no mouse-coloured
virtues; no gradual transitions; all is genius, violence, and
rhapsody, and her thick crowded utterance, often eloquent
and sometimes exquisite, recalls the stammer of a bird
enraptured with life in June. Yet she is not, as this description might imply, sentimentally lyrical, and frequently, if
pardonably, absurd. One of the remarkable qualities of her
work is that she handles the great explosives with complete
good faith. She believes in thunder, violence, genius, and
rhapsody. Therefore, no one is going to sneer at her for
saying so. Moreover, she constantly renews her sense of the
marvellous by touching the earth, if only with the tip of her
toe. She can be sardonic and caustic; she can mention the
stomach.

Why is it, then, that she fails to convince us of the reality
of her romance? It is because her sense of it is more conventional than original. She has taken it from poetry rather
than from life, and from minor poetry more frequently than
from major. She has not, like Meredith, used her freedom

from the ties of realism to reveal something new in the emotions of human beings when they are most roused to excitement. Nor has she gone the other way to work. She has not taken the usual and made it blossom into the extraordinary. When we begin a play by Ibsen we say that there can be nothing romantic about a room with bookcases and upholstered furniture. But in the end we feel that all the forests and nightingales in the world cannot be so romantic as a room with bookcases and upholstered furniture. That is an exaggeration, however; we have overshot the mark. Nightingales and forests are for ever romantic, and it is merely cowardice to be afraid of saying so. But writers are afraid, and very naturally afraid, lest their own feeling for such famous things may not be strong enough to persist against the multitude of other people's feelings. Miss Wilson has no such fear. And thus she has the romantic power of making us feel the stir and tumult of life as a whole. She gives us a general, not a particular, sense of excitement. When at the end of the book Marichaud exclaims: "Life is the thing, Paul. Life is to be the thing," we feel that at last someone has put into words what we have been feeling for two hundred and fifty pages. And to have made us feel that life is the thing for two hundred and fifty pages is a real achievement.

There is no one word, such as romance or realism, to cover, even roughly, the works of Miss Dorothy Richardson. Their chief characteristic, if an intermittent student be qualified to speak, is one for which we still seek a name. She has invented, or, if she has not invented, developed and applied to her own uses, a sentence which we might call the psychological sentence of the feminine gender. It is of a more elastic fibre than the old, capable of stretching to the extreme, of suspending the frailest particles, of enveloping the vaguest shapes. Other writers of the opposite sex have used sentences of this description and stretched them to the extreme. But there is a difference. Miss Richardson has fashioned her sentence consciously, in order that it may descend to the depths and investigate the crannies of Miriam Henderson's consciousness. It is a woman's sentence, but only in the sense that it is used to describe a woman's mind by a writer who is neither proud nor afraid of anything that she may discover in the psychology of her sex. And therefore we feel that the trophies that Miss Richardson brings to the surface, however we may dispute their size, are undoubtedly genuine. Her discoveries are concerned with states of being and not with states of doing. Miriam is aware of "life itself"; of the atmosphere of the table rather than of the table; of the silence rather than of the sound. Therefore she adds an element to her perception of things which has not been noticed before, or, if noticed, has been guiltily suppressed. A man might fall dead at her feet (it is not likely), and Miriam might feel that a violet-coloured ray of light was an important element in her consciousness of the tragedy. If she felt it, she would say it. Therefore, in reading *Revolving Lights* we are often made uncomfortable by feeling that the accent upon the emotions has shifted. What was emphatic is smoothed away. What was important to Maggie Tulliver no longer matters to Miriam Henderson. At first, we are ready to say that nothing is important to Miriam Henderson. That is the way we generally retaliate when an artist tells us that the heart is not, as we should like it to be, a stationary body, but a body which moves perpetually, and is thus always standing in a new relation to the emotions which are the same. Chaucer, Donne, Dickens—each if you read him, shows this change of the heart. That is what Miss Richardson is doing on an infinitely smaller scale. Miriam Henderson is pointing to her heart and saying she feels a pain on her right, and not on her left. She points too didactically. Her pain, compared with Maggie Tulliver's, is a very little pain. But, be that as it may, here we have both Miss Wilson and Miss Richardson proving that the novel is not hung upon a nail and festooned with glory, but, on the contrary, walks the high road, alive and alert, and brushes shoulders with real men and women.

The Obstinate Lady

Review of *The Obstinate Lady*, by W. E. Norris. (1 May, 1919.)

IT is probable that if Mr Norris chose to write down the names of all the novels he can lay claim to they would overflow the allotted page. Even if we had not very pleasant memories of some of them we could infer from internal evidence the long and distinguished ancestry of *The Obstinate Lady*. She has all the marks of maturity: a few, to be frank, of middle age. Mr Norris learnt his craft in the days when a plot was as necessary to a novel as a spring to a mouse-trap; and in these days we have given up catching mice. Yet if it is the plot that teaches this precision and neatness and rightness we need not plume ourselves too much upon our neglect; nor can we deny that a plot of some kind is an admirable device for making us keep our eyes open.

The Obstinate Lady has earned that title because she will not apply for a divorce from the incorrigible drunkard who is her husband. Indeed, when his sins have found him out, she goes to the length of nursing him herself, and to her charge is committed the necessary bottle of morphia. Touched by her conduct, Jack Maddison revokes his will; everything is left to his wife; and next morning his valet finds him dead in his bed. An overdose of morphia is said to be the cause; the widow alone had access to the drug, and the finger of suspicion, though not of blame, must point in her direction. But our sympathies are stirred and enlisted by many other complications. The trap, for it is scarcely a problem, is set down in the middle of a nicely arranged group of English gentle-people. They have a charming house up the river; the only blot upon their circumstances is the unhappy marriage of their daughter and her obstinate refusal to accept her freedom. Nevertheless, they have week-end parties and picnics on the Thames; and they have befriended, a little incongruously, a promising young poet whose verses are said not to rhyme, but that, we suspect, is a concession on Mr Norris's part to the spirit of the age. We rather believe that the war is another of Mr Norris's concessions. There was no war in the Stanfields' England. But it is all so skilfully combined and touched up that the modern additions are almost imperceptible, and the question of Blanche Maddison's guilt is of moment to a good many people whom we know, not intimately indeed, but well enough to feel concerned. Intimacy, of course, is not in Mr Norris's line. His characters keep their distance, and thus it is quite possible for a savage bull on the one hand and a savage review on the other to settle the question of Kitty Stanfield's affections. Grains of sand had no effect upon those rather solid scales. But everything that Mr Norris tells us, whether about a bull or about a review, or about an overdose of morphia has the advantage of being quite possible. That is one of the good results of having proved your skill so often that you know to a hairsbreadth how far it will serve you. And at the right moment, not noisily, or clumsily, or ostentatiously, but quietly and with an appearance of almost humorous ease, the catch is released, and the trap comes down to perfection upon the very tip of the villain's tail.

Mr Norris's Method

Review of *The Triumphs of Sara*, by W. E. Norris.
(4 March, 1920.)

AFTER writing novels for forty years, Mr Norris has given us not merely, as we may guess, forty novels, but an additional volume which has upon the back of it for title W. E. Norris. Although we admit to finding this supernumerary volume always among the best of any author's works, we will at present only extract from it the information that Mr Norris is likely to deprecate enthusiasm as an unnecessary expense of spirit on the part of a reviewer. If we were to offer him incense, he would probably only complain of the smoke. He would point out that above all things he values clearness of sight. Is it not due to his fine stock of this commodity that, after forty years of writing, *The Triumphs of Sara* issues in its turn, firm, competent and kindly, extremely readable, a little cool, and entirely self-possessed?

But clearness of sight is not so common that we can afford to rate its products cheaply. Indeed, we have to own that even with Mr Norris himself dissuading us there was an impulse, half way through this forty-first novel, of dangerous enthusiasm. Lincolnshire; ratting; the Leppingtons of Storr; Uncle Tom asking questions; Jimmy in the Guards; Peggy playing cricket; Aunt Matilda playing patience; Lady Leppington playing the piano; the pleasant country home; the good breeding, the good temper, the good judgment of everyone concerned, did at last produce that warm appreciative mood in the critic which in the kettle precedes, by some five minutes, the hiss and hubbub of boiling over. How this calamity was averted is only to be explained by remarking that an heiress from Manchester called Sara comes upon the scene, and, at her first appearance among the Leppingtons, is convicted by Mr Norris of killing her rat by a fluke. It is an anxious predicament; for a young woman in a novel by Mr Norris must kill something, and if she kills rats by a fluke the presumption is that she

kills men by profession. "From beneath her long lashes she
shot at him one of those glances which she knew by experience found their mark every time she had recourse to
them." That is Sara's form of sport, and, as our quotation
shows, Mr Norris is not altogether at his ease in describing
it. Yet it is amazing and even instructive to observe how
seldom we are allowed to feel any awkwardness. The clear-
sighted and unsentimental relationship between Sara and
Euan Leppington, who, through marriage and separation
and reconciliation, remain good friends, is not only a clever
and truthful performance, but a nice example of a novelist's
economy. Mr Norris is not going to waste his time over the
impossible. He is not going to be rushed off his own neat
strip of indisputable territory. If his characters suffer for it,
suffer they must. No one can complain that they are not
sensible; and Englishwomen are notoriously cold-hearted.
The chief damage that this caution inflicts upon us is that
we can rely so implicitly upon a life-belt when the liner is
torpedoed that, should the kettle boil in the middle of the
chapter, there is no reason to postpone tea. The nuisance of
being torpedoed, as Mr Norris points out, is not that you
are drowned, but that you are rescued "without other
belongings than the clothes on your back". Why we should
complain of feeling safe when Mr Norris is so much better
fitted to deal with safety than with disaster is puzzling,
until, in the crucial scene of the book, we find a reason which
justifies our dissatisfaction. Sara Leppington surprises her
husband alone with Mrs Furness in a Brighton hotel. Now
Mrs Furness loved Euan, and, we submit, had only to say
so rather forcibly in order to send the legitimate wife who
did not love him skulking home in disgrace. As it is, Mrs
Furness is driven off as a small terrier is driven from a large
dog's bone by a horrid outburst of loud meaningless barking. But though a happy ending is assured, and presumably
the desired heir to the Leppington estates, the feeling of
safety rests upon such false foundations that we are more
uneasy than if the whole fabric had been blown sky-high
before our eyes.

   This conclusion, however, need only be reached if you
wish to come to a conclusion, if, that is to say, you stray off

Mr Norris's land on to debatable territory where he makes no pretence to rule. Stay within his precincts and you are still perfectly safe.

Mr Norris's Standard

Review of *Tony the Exceptional*, by W. E. Norris.
(10 February, 1921.)

MR NORRIS has now been writing novels, his publishers tell us, for forty years, and *Tony the Exceptional* is, we believe, the youngest of a family of fifty, or it may be sixty, for we shall not perjure ourselves by pretending that we have kept strict count, or pretend that we could recite a large proportion of their names offhand. For all that, whenever we meet with one of the short, safe, amiably patronizing reviews with which Mr Norris is annually saluted, we want to tell him that we feel, and would, if we could, explain, that he is somehow different from the rest. We may treat him like an old established firm of grocers. We may open the familiar parcel and sniff the contents and say that it is up to sample, a trifle paler, pinker, smaller or rounder than last year's product, but that is only because the reviewers of novels are the laziest and most perfunctory of mortals, and because, to tell the truth, the task of analysing what we mean when we say that Mr Norris is different from the rest is difficult. One has, in the first place, to strike the right pitch. One must resist the temptation to make a discovery of Mr Norris. He is not so great an artist as Flaubert nor so fine a psychologist as Henry James. No; but having shut off the high-lights with one hand one must be equally quick to shut off the shadows with the other. He has no sort of truck with the obscene creatures of the underworld—the mere manufacturers of stuffing. His station, preserved so long with what has come to appear such patient modesty, is precisely in that mid-region between the obscure and the illustrious, where it is most difficult to distinguish clearly. Let us see what we can make out by the light of *Tony the Exceptional*.

The publishers having said that the book is "well up to Mr Norris's standard—he tells a fascinating story in a straightforward style", we feel impelled to say that far too much attention is paid to Mr Norris's fascinating stories and far too little to the art with which he tells them. The story as it happens is a good one; it mystifies, interests, and works out; but the style is not straightforward if simple, common, or easy to come by is meant by that. Indeed, when one says that Mr Norris is different from the rest, one means largely that he has a gift unfortunately rare among us—a sense of form. No one acquires that sense because he happens to hit upon a good anecdote, or the police-court records would make the best reading in the world. The 280 pages of *Tony* are the result of innumerable acts of selection; the hand that shaped them was inspired by a definite artistic aim. For purely aesthetic reasons which have nothing to do with the story, now this has been left out, now that has been put in. If we ask what Mr Norris has left out, it is easy to reply hurriedly, "Oh, everything interesting". He has left out passion, tragedy, philosophy, psychology, and so on. And what has he put in? Again the answer would be hasty—"Oh, ladies and gentlemen", meaning by that manners, the manners of good society.

Tony the Exceptional does, on the face of it, lend some support to this view, inasmuch as every one concerned in it is either a lady or a gentleman, and therefore of good manners, or an ex-shop assistant, and therefore of bad. Never were heights and contours more plainly marked upon a survey map than are the shades of good and bad breeding in a novel by Mr Norris. The serious charge against a novelist of manners is, of course, that he allows himself to be put off by surface tricks which human beings have adopted to decorate or facilitate the rub of daily life. In another hundred years, one might argue, the code will have changed, and where then will be the point of Mr Norris's ladies and gentlemen? Have they not already rather the look of Orientals going through mysterious devotions, prostrating themselves before dusty top hats, obsolete dress clothes, and ancient packs of visiting cards? Doris, for example, will not marry the man she loves because he has told her a lie. She does not consider that lies differ, that liars may be pitiable, that characters are complex. No lady marries a liar; that is her code; and to that she adheres. But she has somehow evolved for herself a dispensation which decrees that if a lady has scratched her initials upon a sixpenny-bit she may, upon delivery of the coin at the critical moment, revoke her decision without compromising her honour. Was there ever an idol made more palpably of wood?

But we have overshot the mark by a long way, as it is not difficult to do, indeed, where the marks are so lightly scored. The situation which we have just declared to be absurd is, as a matter of fact, the most interesting in the book, and the one we should certainly select for analysis if we wished to explain our belief that Mr Norris is not a time-serving, mechanical writer, but a writer of art and intuition. Doris and her code and her sixpence are, we say, absurd. Without disputing the matter Mr Norris quietly goes on to persuade us that Doris is much more pitiable than ridiculous. She knows that she is absurd; she is afraid of her own absurdity. She is a self-contained and rigid character. It is not in her nature to talk and analyse. A sixpence with initials scratched upon it is as near as she can come to self-expression. We are not asked to admire her. Why, even her mother, who adores her, says a little later that she herself cannot influence Doris. "I don't say that she's right, I only say that she's like that." It drips out, as if by chance, that mother and daughter never have much to say to each other. Indeed, the mother is a little afraid of her daughter. Thus we are brought to see that Doris is "like that". But only a true novelist does it in this way—one scene suggesting and confirming another spontaneously, as bubbles froth at the end of a pipe. And each has sprung not from observation of manners but from insight into the human heart.

A skilful critic might from this point go on to determine why it is that Mr Norris never persists but always draws back with a smile from exploring these moments of intuition. It is difficult not to speak as though his discretion were due to that social tact which he finds so admirable in his characters. To know people intimately one must pursue them into the privacy of their rooms. But Mr Norris is never alone with themselves. There is always a dog upon the hearth-rug. Yet we are inclined to think that it is not a modest estimate of his own powers that restrains him. He obeys a mysterious law which, without knowing exactly what we mean, we call the law of form. The demands of a good story probably help to guide his steps. A love of clean language forbids riot or indiscretion in that department. A moderate, or even slightly cynical, view of human nature checks exuberance of another kind. In short, we would as soon read Mr Norris on a railway journey as a good French novelist, and for much the same reasons. But pending the decisions of the skilful critic we may let Mr Norris, in a characteristic sentence, sum up what we feel to be the supporting backbone of all his fiction—". . . when you have a standard you have a standard, and there is no use in arguing about it".

A Real American

Review of *Free and Other Stories*, and *Twelve Men*, by Theodore Dreiser. (21 August, 1919.)

AMERICAN literature is still terribly apt to excite the snobbish elements in an English critic. It is either feeble with an excess of culture, or forcible with a self-conscious virility. In either case it appears to be influenced by the desire to conciliate or flout the European standards; and such deference not only never attains its object, but, perhaps deservedly, brings its own punishment in the shape of patronage and derision. One cannot help, on such occasions, boasting of the English descent from Shakespeare. At first sight Mr Dreiser appears to be another of those pseudo-Europeans whose productions may pass muster across the Atlantic, but somehow look over here like careful copies from the old masters. There are many stories, we should suppose, neither better nor worse and indeed much resembling "Free" in the current magazines. But what we should expect an English writer to rattle off with some dash and self-confidence, the American writer produces slowly, languidly, with much fumbling for words and groping for subtleties which seem to escape him. The end is apparent long before it is reached, and we come to it in a listless straggling way which makes the whole expedition seem rather pointless. As there is perhaps no more fatiguing form of mental exercise than the reading of short stories told without zest, the prospect of ten more to come descended like a mist upon the horizon. The cloud lifted, however, against all expectation, as a dull day gets finer and finer without one's seeing exactly where the light comes from. While we were growing more and more conscious that Mr Dreiser lacked all the necessary qualities for a writer of short stories—concentration, penetration, form—unconsciously we were reading on at a great rate and enjoying the book considerably. At a certain point then it was necessary to come to terms with Mr Dreiser and to inform him that, if he would consent to drop his claim to be a writer of short

stories, we for our part would renounce our privileges as the
lineal descendants of Shakespeare.

And yet what did our pleasure come from? It did not
come from the usual sources; it did not come from excitement or shock; it came, as if surreptitiously, from a sense of
American fields and American men and women and of
America herself, gross, benevolent, and prolific. For some
hundreds of years, of course, the existence of America has
been a well-known fact; but the lettered classes have kept
their country in the background, or presented it in a form
suited to European taste. Mr Dreiser, however, appears to
be so much of an American that he describes it without
being aware that he is doing anything of the kind. In the
same way a home-bred child describes the family in which
he has been brought up. There is little evidence that Mr
Dreiser has been influenced by Europe. He is not percept-
ibly cultivated. His taste seems to be bad. When he describes
an artist, we, on the other hand, see a journalist.

> Davies swelled with feeling. The night, the tragedy, the
> grief, he saw it all. But also with the cruel instinct of the
> budding artist, that he already was, he was beginning to
> meditate on the character of story it would make—the colour,
> the pathos. "I'll get it all in!" he exclaimed, feelingly, if
> triumphantly, at last. "I'll get it all in!"

Mr Dreiser gets a great deal too much of it in, but, together
with the colour and the pathos, there is another quality
which excuses his sins of taste, and perhaps explains them.
He has genuine vitality. His interest in life, when not impeded by the restrictions of a definite form, bubbles and
boils over and produces *Twelve Men*, a much more interesting work than *Free*.

Whether we are able to recognize the originals or not,
these twelve character sketches are extremely readable.
And to an English reader they are, besides, rather strange.
With superficial differences, each of these men is of a large,
opulent, masterful character. Each is, as Mr Dreiser defines
it, "free", with "the real spiritual freedom where the mind,
as it were, stands up and looks at itself, faces Nature unafraid, is aware of its own weaknesses, its strengths . . . kicks

dogma out of doors, and yet deliberately and of choice holds fast to many, many simple and human things, and rounds out life, or would, in a natural, normal, courageous, healthy way". One of these men writes songs, another directs companies, a third builds toy engines. They are all busy and engrossed, and in love with life. Yet with all their power they seem childish—childish in their love of fame, in their love of mankind, in their sentimentality and simplicity. One is certain that their songs will be bad ones, their pictures melodramatic, their stories mere journalism. But their animal spirits are superb. Nor are they entirely animal. The abundance of life in their veins overflows into all kinds of fine and friendly relations with their fellows. Mr Dreiser describes them with such enthusiasm that his work has a character of its own—an American character. He is not himself by any means a great writer, but he may be the stuff from which, in another hundred years or so, great writers will be born.

Sonia Married

Review of *Sonia Married*, by Stephen McKenna.
(28 August, 1919.)

IF anyone wishes to take the measure of Mr Stephen
McKenna's *Sonia Married* by the rough method of comparison, let him recall the once famous *Dodo* of Mr E. F.
Benson. Sonia is another of those irresistible chattering up-
to-date ladies who compel the most surly to tolerate and
even to forgive by talking at dinner-parties at the tops of
their voices in the following manner: "Tell him [her hus-
band] that I shall elope to Sloane-square—I don't believe
anyone's ever eloped to Sloane-square, but its the handiest
place in the world; even the Hounslow and Barking non-
stop train stops there—so sweet of them I always think—I
shall go there with Peter and live in his flat and star in
revue . . ." and so on. Remembering that the female dodo
implies a male, it is easy to infer that the husband admires
his wife's wit and is a simple-hearted trustful fellow with
ideas and aspirations which keep him at home while she
dines out. He thinks it very right that other men should
admire her, and when the crash comes, he used, if memory
serves us, after displaying a gentlemanly toleration, to be
killed in the hunting-field. But Mr McKenna is painstak-
ingly modern; and he has done his best to bring his version
up to date. David O'Rane has been blinded in the early days
of the war, and now believes in social reform, loving one's
neighbour, and trusting one's wife. He has a habit of sitting
on the floor stroking the head of a Saint Bernard dog, while
he talks sometimes with "cold vibrant passion", and sometimes with boyish eagerness about the future of England.
". . . Its got to stand for a good deal more than it did before
the war; we owe it to the fellows who have died and the
fellows who are dying now."

His contribution to the problem is to turn a very large
room in his house on the Embankment into what his wife's
family and friends call a "casual ward" or a "doss house".
By this they mean that the door is unlocked, and anyone

who chooses can come in and eat cake in front of a large fire.
It is chiefly used by Members of Parliament and a consumptive pacifist in an orange-coloured tie, who, though
extremely voluble, seem highly respectable, and in no
particular need of a cake. But on one occasion O'Rane, in
his unworldly way, brought home a drunken soldier whom
he had found in the street. The man was an officer, the visit
lasted only one night, but "it was the last straw for Sonia".
She went off with one of the Members of Parliament; and
O'Rane, forgetting that he had said on page 78 that if his
wife fell in love with another man and ran away with him
he would not want to stop her, forgetting, moreover, his
own conduct with a lady secretary, behaves as if he had
never read a line of Shelley or professed any love for his
neighbour. The deplorable truth is that he chases, or
believes that he chases, the consumptive pacifist violently
about the room. The real malefactor, Mr Grayle, M.P., is
soundly drubbed by another elderly politician, who, in
telling the story, remarks, "His one weak point was the
injured knee, and I concentrated my attack on that."

These unpleasantnesses would no doubt melt into a rose-
tinted mist if the boyish charm of O'Rane and the irresistible fascination of Sonia had done their work. Without such
an anaesthetic the operation of reading is full of painful little
shocks as if one kept on waking up in the middle of having a
tooth out. Their conduct, if one looks at it with open eyes,
seems alternately frivolous and bestial. But, to do Mr
McKenna justice, his concern is not with the conduct of his
characters but with their conversation. He manages to
keep that going all the time, if not brilliantly, still with
remarkable smartness, considering how much they talk and
how easily the psychological complexities of the O'Ranes
might have been disposed of in half a dozen words. The war
is very cleverly rigged up in the background—Mr Asquith
resigns; Lord Kitchener is drowned; and the battles of the
drawing-room are represented with great verisimilitude.
One keeps asking oneself "Who can the Duchess of Ross be
meant for?" or "Which of our peeresses looks like 'a lioness
that has been rolling in French chalk'?" This amounts to
saying that *Sonia Married* runs every chance of great

popularity; and if we have omitted to praise the skill, deft-
ness, and smartness of the story it must be that we are perhaps a little shocked to find that the dodo is by no means
extinct.

Winged Phrases

Review of *Avowals*, by George Moore. (30 October, 1919.)

NO one, perhaps, has ever spent a pleasant evening talking about books without wondering why it is that the things that are said are so much better than the things that are written. One reason will occur to most people; enthusiasm, which is the life-blood of criticism, tells in tone and manner, for or against, rightly or wrongly, with a conviction and sincerity which are unmistakable yet scarcely to be preserved, save by the rare masters of expression, in print. And where there is warmth of feeling, everything else, it seems, easily follows—the nicest discriminations, the most daring conjectures, illuminations and felicities clustering one on top of another like blue and purple soap bubbles at the end of a pipe, and, like bubbles, breaking and vanishing. Mr Moore has a much better phrase for the ardours of conversation when he speaks of Banville "throwing winged phrases into the air that, rising with rapid wing-beats, floated, wheeled, and chased each other like birds whose pastime is flying". But to cut the matter short, here is Mr George Moore talking about books, and giving us the most delightful example of printed talk that we can remember to have met with in English—if, indeed, it be in English. One chapter is actually written in French; the others, as Henry James said of one of Mr Moore's novels, seem to be translated from that language. Not, of course, that Mr Moore is anything but a master of his own tongue, which is presumably the Irish. It is the thinking, or, more obscurely, the atmosphere, that seems to be in French; and had we not express evidence to the contrary we should imagine that these conversations took place in a Parisian café, at a little round table, with a glass of his favourite chocolate in front of him, rather than in the "long narrow slum" of Ebury-street, or in the Georgian solidity of Regent's Park.

For the first two conversations are with Mr Gosse, and Mr Moore's theme is that "English prose narrative is the weakest part of our literature". A casual remark made

somewhere by Mr Gosse that "English genius had gone into
poetry" had started Mr Moore upon the toils of composition; when, the door opening and the maid announcing Mr
Gosse, he threw himself into the far more congenial task of
conversation. Such is the setting. But if anyone will momentarily recall the course of a conversation when both the
talkers have the theme by heart, can toss the ball where
they like, and return the lightest or wildest flick of the
other's racquet, he will agree that any report by a third
person is valueless. Besides, one of the great merits of such
conversation is that it proves nothing. Whether Mr Moore
proved his case against prose fiction we do not remember.
Our impression is that he danced round that stout matron
with elfish vivacity, assuring her that her place was at the
wash-tub and her demeanour of a plebeian stolidity out of
all keeping with the incorrigible triviality of her mind;
when, having made her look both flustered and foolish, he
suddenly transformed her into a slim and shapely goddess
and fell at her feet in an ecstasy of adoration. This is neither
a full nor an accurate report. In the course of an undulating
dialogue which meanders in and out, round and round the
feet of Fielding, Thackeray, Dickens and Trollope, they are
all, for one reason or another, found wanting, lacking in
breeding, in depth, in seriousness, in sensibility; but suddenly he stops himself short; there is one English novelist
whose wine is of the purest—Jane Austen. There is one
scene in one of her books where "we find the burning
human heart in English prose narrative for the first and,
alas, for the last time". The book is *Sense and Sensibility*; the
scene we will not specify, for most people will like nothing
better than to find it for themselves, and enjoy nothing
more than to hear Mr Moore praise it for them.

Then we rush on, it matters not how, to the question of
names, and if you reflect what our novelists are called you
will no longer be surprised by the mediocrity of what they
have written.

Trollope! Did ever anybody bear a name that predicted a
style more trollopy. Anthony, too, in front of it, to make
matters worse. And Walter Scott is a jog-trot name, a round-

faced name, a snub-nosed, spectacled, pot-bellied name, a
placid, beneficent, worthy old bachelor name; a name that
evokes all conventional ideas and formulas, a Grub Street
name, an old oak and Abbotsford name; a name to improvise
novels to buy farms with. And Thackeray is a name for a
footman, for the syllables clatter like plates, and when we
hear it we say, We shall want the carriage at half-past 2,
Thackeray.

We have broken a vow which we made not to quote from
Mr Moore, and we are now punished; for to interrupt Mr
Moore is as barbarous as to silence the nightingale. Mr
Gosse alone is able to do it. From time to time Mr Gosse
recalls him to the matter in hand, or suggests that the
drawing-room window, in front of which they are sitting,
had better be closed. But Mr Gosse has his place in the
composition. He serves to define Mr Moore. He brings out
the fact that we are hearing the voice of a fallible, frivolous,
occasionally aggravating, elderly gentleman who will not
refrain from poking fun at the Athenaeum Club, or at any
other object that takes his fancy. And is it not because the
fallible human being is absent in most books of criticism
that we learn so little from them? Such is human imperfec-
tion that to love one thing you are almost constrained to
hate another. Far from suppressing this natural lopsided-
ness, Mr Moore indulges it, avows it, and carries us away
on the breath of his preference. We have not listened long
to the brilliant and often beautiful denunciation of English
prose narrative before we perceive that our companion, if
we may call him so, is heading for some favourite landmark.
One scans the horizon for the first sight of it. Can it be in
Germany? In France much more probably. But surely he
cannot altogether ignore Russia! One tries to remember the
date of Mr Moore's birth. It was *Esther Waters*, one reflects, that first made one look up and down the bookshelves
for another book with the name of George Moore on the
back of it. We were always, perhaps, a little disappointed
after *Esther Waters*. The language was abundant and
flexible, the rhythm of the most musical fluidity; what was
wanting? Concentration or intensity was it? Some power,

perhaps, of getting outside himself, or forgetting all about himself? And then George Moore is not a good name for a novelist; and now we recollect that it is above all things a philosophical name. Whatever the reason, nothing came up to *Esther Waters*, until the autobiographies began; and still they seem to us the very best autobiographies in the Irish language, for the soft cadence in which they are written is Irish and has nothing whatever to do with English. But while we are thus musing, Mr Moore has reached his goal; he is prostrate before his idol; and it is of course, Turgenev. But we must not call him Turgenev.

> Ivan Tourguéneff. Hearken, reader, to the musical syllables—Ivan Tourguéneff; repeat them again and again, and before long the Fates coiled in their elusive draperies in the British Museum will begin to rise up before your eyes; the tales of the great Scythian tale-teller are as harmonious as they, and we ask in vain why the Gods should have placed the light of Greece in the hands of a Scythian.

These words are the prelude to a hymn of praise so sincere and so inspiring that, whatever our own view of Turgenev, we feel that we know him better because we have seen him through the eyes of someone who loves him. Yet love which springs from so profound a source almost necessarily brings with it an instinctive jealousy: for unconsciously so much of ourselves is in whatever we love. So Mr Moore, believing that since the world began there have been only two tale-tellers, Balzac and Turgenev, and that Turgenev is the greater of the two, is necessarily and sincerely unjust.

> Tolstoy writes with a mind as clear as an electric lamp, a sizzling white light, crude and disagreeable, and Flaubert's writing is as beautiful as marquetry, or was thought to be so once. Be this as it may, he is no tale-teller; his best books are not novels, but satires. There is Huysmans with *En Route*, and the Goncourts have written interesting pages, which some future generation may glance at curiously. There have been men of genius who wrote novels, Dostoieffsky, for instance; but vapours and tumult do not make tales, and before we can admire them modern life must wring all the Greek out of us.

His farrago is wonderful, but I am not won. Maupassant wrote perfect tales, but they are so very little.

We must find another word than the word "unjust" to describe a judgment which one may think jealous or capricious, but which we cannot deny, urged as it is by a fervid conviction, to be both penetrating and true. Let us read on a little farther in the conversation with Mr Balderston:

> I admire Tolstoy; but if I only dared—I beg of you, he interrupted. Well, I continued, Gautier used to boast that the visible world was visible to him, but to no one was it ever so visible as it is to Tolstoy. His eyesight exceeds all eyesight before or since. At this point I paused, and my visitor and I sat looking at each other, myself very much abashed. . . . What is your conclusion? That Tolstoy is not a great psychologist, I answered tremblingly, for when he comes to speak of the soul he is no longer certain; he doesn't know. But I'm saying something that no one will agree with, that no one has ever said.

That is memorable and stimulating criticism because, even if one had not read the praises of Turgenev which precede and partly inspire it, one would know that it is the fruit not of coldness, but of love. The love of art which is the light that Mr Moore carries with him through all the libraries in the world wavers and flickers, gutters and splutters, but never goes out. The pages, the faces, of Pater and Mallarmé, of Rudyard Kipling and Henry James, are alike lit up— partially, of course, leaving great tracts of them in shadow, but so warmly and brightly that we know that if we cannot see what Mr Moore sees for ourselves, it exists somewhere for him. The faces crowd and cluster, but among them all we see most vividly the engrossed and ardent countenance of the writer himself, hanging absorbed over the pages of others, weaving with infinite delicacy and toil a new page of his own. Truly, we can conjure up no more exhilarating and encouraging spectacle than the spectacle of Mr George Moore, who declares himself an Ishmael and an outcast in England, determining that he will live to the age of ninety in order that he may be able to write English prose "nearly as well as I should like to be able to write it".

A Born Writer

Review of *Esther Waters*, by George Moore. (29 July, 1920.)

AFTER many years *Esther Waters* appears again, entirely revised, and with an introduction which, to our disappointment, has more to say about Irish politics than about English fiction. Whether any critic of those days predicted a long life for the book we know not. At what date it was written and what views the author had in mind we are not told. At any rate in the summer of 1920 it sets out again; and whether for a long voyage and by reason of what qualities it has survived so far the critics of today must make up their minds. That is not easy. For it is a quiet book, and an old-fashioned rather than an old book. About a century ago it was the habit of novelists to produce masterpieces which were known for such from the moment of birth. *Waverley*, *Pickwick*, and *Jane Eyre* are all cases in point. The public applauded and the critics clapped hands with them unanimously. Later, for reasons which it would lead us astray to discuss, the process of recognition was much more gradual and difficult, and far from acclaiming at the outset the public had to be coaxed and even coerced before it would tolerate. But *Esther Waters* belongs neither to one class nor to the other. It was neither admitted a classic from the start nor has it fought a battle, won a victory, and founded a school. Somehow it has come through the press of the struggle by qualities which are not so easy to define.

Leaving aside such obvious merits as the story, which is varied and interesting, and the style, which, with occasional spaces of melody and charm, is invariably lucid and effortless, it seems as if the book's virtue lay in a shapeliness which is at once admirable and disconcerting. The novel begins with the sentence, "She stood on the platform watching the receding train". A few pages before the end the sentence recurs. Esther Waters stands once more on the platform watching the receding train. Once more a servant's oblong box, painted a reddish brown, is on the seat beside her. Between these two appearances eighteen years have passed, eighteen years of labour, suffering, and disappointment. A great deal had happened, so much that she could not remember it all. The situations she had been in; her life with that dear, good soul, Miss Rice; then Fred Parsons; then William again! her marriage, the life in the public-house, money lost and money won, heartbreakings, death, everything that could happen had happened to her.

But the recurring scene is not a formal device to reduce the varied incidents of her life to symmetry. All through Mr Moore has curbed himself to this particular ending, renouncing this, insisting upon that, allowing himself few or none of the licences and redundances in which English novelists luxuriate. The life of a servant girl is a long series of sordid drudgeries scattered with scant pleasures; and thus he has presented it, without taking refuge in sentiment or in romance. Throughout the names are insignificant; the places (with the exception of Woodview, and there we are limited to the kitchen and the pantry) without charm; while the fates above preserve blank faces in the discharge of their duties. No one is allowed either sensational reprieve or sensational disaster. A number of writers have outdone Mr Moore in the force with which they depict poverty and misery, but they have failed to penetrate beyond their day because they have always dashed the picture from their hands in an access of indignation or clouded it with tears. They have rarely had his power of maintaining that in art life needs neither condemnation nor justification. The story owes much of its buoyancy and permanency to the fact that we can examine it dispassionately. There it hangs, complete, apart. Yet by this we do not mean that there is no morality to be found in it; for when Mr Moore calls Esther Waters "as characteristically English as 'Don Quixote' is Spanish", he means perhaps that in the person of Esther he has laid bare honesty, fidelity, courage, and has made these, the Saxon virtues, rather than the charms and subtleties of the Latins, the leading qualities in the drama. But he himself remains invisible.

Vivid, truthful, so lightly and yet so firmly constructed as it is, what then prevents us from talking of immortality and greatness? In one word, the quality of the emotion.

Although in retrospect there is not a single scene that lacks animation, or a single character clumsily or conventionally portrayed, both scenes and characters are nevertheless curiously flat. The dialogue is always toneless and monotonous. The conception springs from no deep original source, and the execution has that sort of evenness which we see in the work of a highly sensitive student copying on to his canvas the picture of some great master. If that is the reason why *Esther Waters* does not affect us directly as a more imperfect but more original work is capable of doing, we cannot deny that it holds a very distinguished place in English fiction. Moreover, though the public will always prefer both Shakespeare and Mrs Henry Wood, *Esther Waters* will go on being read and re-read with peculiar interest by those who attempt the art of novel writing themselves. For, when all is said and done, Mr Moore is a born writer; and, though great novelists are rare, of how many people in a generation can one say truthfully that?

Cleverness and Youth

Review of *Limbo*, by Aldous Huxley. (5 February, 1920.)

WE know for ourselves that Mr Huxley is very clever; and his publisher informs us that he is young. For both these reasons his reviewers may pay him the compliment, and give themselves the pleasure, of taking him seriously. Instead, that is, of saying that there are seven short stories in *Limbo* which are all clever, amusing, and well written, and recommending the public to read them, as we can conscientiously do, we are tempted to state, what it is so seldom necessary to state, that short stories can be a great deal more than clever, amusing, and well written. There is another adjective—"interesting"; that is the adjective we should like to bestow upon Mr Huxley's short stories, for it is the best worth having.

The difficulty is that in order to be interesting, as we define the word, Mr Huxley would have to forgo, or go beyond, many of the gifts which nature and fortune have put in his way. Merely to skim the quotations in "Richard Greenow" and the rest is to perceive that Mr Huxley is extremely well read; then he has evidently first-hand knowledge of a great public school, which he calls Aesop; and of an Oxford college, which he calls Canteloup; moreover, whatever the intellectual fad of the metropolis, he is fated to know both its professors and its disciples. His eyes have opened perforce upon the follies of the upper middle classes and the unfortunate physical infirmities of the *intelligentsia*. This is none of Mr Huxley's fault, but it is a little his misfortune, and it is better worth attention since so many of the young and the clever of our country are inevitably in the same case. To have named the reading of books as an obstacle to the writing of stories needs some explanation. We hold no brief for the simple peasant. Yet we cannot help thinking that it is well to leave a mind under a counterpane of moderate ignorance; it grows more slowly, but being more slowly exposed it avoids that excessive surface sensibility which wastes the strength of the precocious. Again,

to be aware too soon of sophisticated society makes it tempt-
ing for a young writer to use his first darts in attack and
derision. If he is as dexterous and as straightforward as Mr
Huxley the attack is an inspiriting spectacle. Humbug seems
to collapse, pretension to be pricked. Here is the portrait of a
fellow of Canteloup,

> who had had the most dazzling academic career of his
> generation. . . . Mr Glottenham did not prepossess at a first
> glance; the furrows of his face were covered with a short grey
> sordid stubble; his clothes were disgusting with the spilth of
> many years of dirty feeding; he had the shoulders and long
> hanging arms of an ape—an ape with a horribly human look
> about it. When he spoke it was like the sound of a man break-
> ing coke; he spoke incessantly and on every subject. His know-
> ledge was enormous; but he possessed the secret of a strange
> inverted alchemy—he knew how to turn the richest gold to
> lead, could make the most interesting topic so intolerably
> tedious that it was impossible, when he talked, not to loathe it.

There is an equally amusing description of a dinner with
the Headmaster of Aesop and Mrs Crawister, a lady of
"swelling port" and unexpected utterance, who talks to the
bewildered boys now about eschatology, now about Manx
cats ("No tails, no tails, like men. How symbolical everything is!"), now about the unhappy fate of the carrion crow,
who mates for life. It is amusing; it is perhaps true; and yet
as one reads one cannot help exclaiming that English
society is making it impossible to produce English literature. Write about boots, one is inclined to say, about coins,
sea anemones, crayfish—but, as you value your life, steer
clear of the English upper middle classes. They lie, apparently, so open to attack, they are undoubtedly such an
obstacle to vision; but their openness is the openness of the
tiger's jaw which ends by swallowing you whole and leaving
no trace. Happily, "Ever After" is but another proof of their
rapacity. Mr Huxley sets out to kill a great many despicable
conventions, and to attack a large and disgusting schoolmaster. But having laughed at the conventions and the
schoolmaster, they suddenly turn the tables on him. Now,
they seem to say, talk about something that you do believe

in—and behold, Mr Huxley can only stammer. Love and death, like damp fireworks, refuse to flare up in such an atmosphere, and as usual the upper middle classes escape unhurt.

But with Mr Huxley it is only necessary to wait a little longer; and we can wait without anxiety. He is not merely clever, well read, and honest, but when he forgets himself he discovers very charming things. The best story—barring "Happy Families," a play, which, after two readings, we understand insufficiently to pronounce upon—is not a story at all, but a description of an interview in a book-shop. He opens a book of fashion plates.

> Beauties in crinolines swam with the amplitude of pavilioned ships across the pages. Their feet were represented as thin and flat and black, like tea-leaves shyly protruding from under their petticoats. . . . And it occurred to me then that if I wanted an emblem to picture the sacredness of marriage and the influence of the home, I could not do better than choose two little black feet like tea-leaves peeping out decorously from under the hem of wide, disguising petticoats. While heels and thoroughbred insteps should figure—oh well, the reverse.

And then he sees a piano—"the yellow keys grinned at me in the darkness like the teeth of an ancient horse". Emboldened by our pleasure in such good writing as this, we would admonish Mr Huxley to leave social satire alone, to delete the word "incredibly" from his pages, and to write about interesting things that he likes. Nobody ever takes advice; even so, we hazard the opinion that Mr Huxley's next book will be not only clever, amusing, and well written, but interesting into the bargain.

Freudian Fiction

Review of *An Imperfect Mother*, by J. D. Beresford.
(25 March, 1920.)

MR BERESFORD is always a conscientious writer, but in *An Imperfect Mother* one cannot help feeling that conscience can at best play a stepmother's part in the art of fiction. She can keep things neat and orderly, see that no lies are told, and bring up her stepchildren to lead strenuous and self-respecting lives. But the joys of intimacy are not hers; there is something perfunctory in the relationship. In this case we hazard the opinion that, from the highest motives, Mr Beresford has acted the part of stepfather to some of the very numerous progeny of Dr Freud. The chief characters, Cecilia, Stephen, and Margaret Weatherley, are his children and not Mr Beresford's. On page 12 there is certain proof of it:

> Something within him had inarticulately protested against his conscientious endeavours to submit himself to the idea of this new ambition. . . . He had been harassed, too, by a persistent nightmare, quite new in his experience—a nightmare of being confined in some intolerably dark and restricted place from which he struggled desperately to break out. Sometimes he had succeeded, and waked with a beautiful sense of relief.

After that one expects to find that Stephen is beginning, unconsciously, to fall in love with the schoolmaster's daughter; nor is one surprised to discover that he is the victim of an unacknowledged passion for his mother. It follows that she returns his affection in the inarticulate manner of those who lived before Freud, and, finding herself supplanted by Margaret Weatherley, decided to run away with Threlfall the organist. This is strictly in accordance with the new psychology, which in the sphere of medicine claims to have achieved positive results of great beneficence. A patient who has never heard a canary sing without falling down in a fit can now walk through an avenue of cages without a twinge of emotion since he has faced the fact that his mother kissed him in his cradle. The triumphs of science are beautifully positive. But for novelists the matter is much more complex; and should they, like Mr Beresford, possess a conscience, the question how far they should allow themselves to be influenced by the discoveries of the psychologists is by no means simple. Happily, that is their affair; our task in reviewing is comparatively easy, although we, too, are conscious of a division of mind which twenty or even ten years ago could hardly have afflicted our predecessors. Stated briefly, our dilemma resolves itself into this. Judged as an essay in morbid psychology, *An Imperfect Mother* is an interesting document; judged as a novel, it is a failure. All this talk, we find ourselves protesting when Mr Beresford in his able way describes Medboro', or the building of a factory, is irrelevant to the case. We cannot help adopting the professional manner of a doctor intent upon his diagnosis. A love scene interests us because something bearing significantly upon our patient's state of mind may emerge. Our attention is rewarded.

> She laughed at his deliberation. "You *are* a funny boy," she chided him. "One might think I was your mother." . . . The reference used as a simile finished Stephen. The obscure resistance that he had been fighting to overcome was no longer physical inertia; it had become a positive impulse.

Yes, says the scientific side of the brain, that is interesting; that explains a great deal. No, says the artistic side of the brain, that is dull and has no human significance whatever. Snubbed and discouraged, the artist retreats; and before the end of the book the medical man is left in possession of the field; all the characters have become cases; and our diagnosis is now so assured that a boy of six has scarcely opened his lips before we detect in him unmistakable symptoms of the prevailing disease.

There remains the question whether we are not pandering to some obsolete superstition when we thus decree that certain revelations are of medical significance, others of human; that some are only fit for the columns of the *Lancet*, others for the pages of fiction. If it is true that our conduct in crucial moments is immensely influenced, if not decided, by some forgotten incident in childhood, then surely it is cowardice on the part of the novelist to persist in ascribing our behaviour to untrue causes. We must protest that we do not wish to debar Mr Beresford from making use of any key that seems to him to fit the human mind. Our complaint is rather that in *An Imperfect Mother* the new key is a patent key that opens every door. It simplifies rather than complicates, detracts rather than enriches. The door swings open briskly enough, but the apartment to which we are admitted is a bare little room with no outlook whatever. Partly, no doubt, this is to be attributed to the difficulty of adapting ourselves to any new interpretation of human character; but partly, we think, to the fact that, in the ardours of discovery, Mr Beresford has unduly stinted his people of flesh and blood. In becoming cases they have ceased to be individuals.

Revolution

Review of *Revolution*, by J. D. Beresford. (27 January, 1921.)

IF the reader finds something amiss with Mr Beresford's *Revolution* he will probably blame the subject. He will say that revolutions are not a fit subject for fiction. And there he will be wrong. But, as we should probably allow if we had him in the armchair opposite, we can see what he means. He means that to write a book about what is going to happen in England when Isaac Perry proclaims a general strike and the Army refuses to obey its officers is not a novelist's business. He feels, and here we agree with him, a little defrauded when a writer like Mr Beresford, who can make you interested in his characters, chooses instead to make you interested in the failure of the Communal milk-cart to arrive at Winston at half-past nine. Yet the fault cannot lie with revolutions. As Tolstoy and Hardy have proved, revolutions are fine things to write about if only they have happened sufficiently long ago. But if you are impelled to invent your own revolution, half your energy will be needed to make sure that it works. A large part of Mr Beresford's labour in writing *Revolution* has been spent, we should guess, upon calculations, of which we invent the following example. If the N.U.R. came out on Thursday is it probable that the Transport Workers would follow suit on Monday morning, and, if so, what would be the effect on the Stock Exchange, and how much would the pound sterling have fallen in New York by the following Friday? The calculation is difficult. Moreover, we have observed that when such arguments are seriously discussed the disputants simplify their labours by using letters of the alphabet instead of proper names. It would be untrue to say that the young soldier Paul Leaming, his father the merchant, his sister the woman at home, Isaac Perry the trade union leader, Lord Fynemore the aristocrat, are merely letters of the alphabet, but they are far more alphabetical than we like.

We go back, in a digression which the eminence of Mr Beresford's name perhaps sanctions, to wonder what has happened to the author of *Jacob Stahl*, the *House in Demetrius-road* and *These Lynnekers*, to name three very memorable novels out of a total now amounting to fourteen. We say offhand that he is becoming increasingly intellectual and add, by way of explanation, that we find him more and more inclined to think about life and less and less inclined to feel about it. He now seems impelled to write a new novel by the desire to see whether a theory which works correctly in the study will set human legs and arms in motion and even affect the action of the human heart. He is immune, we feel, from all sorts of distractions and beguilements and grows increasingly accurate, methodical and explicit. Thus in *Revolution* it is the intellectual efficiency of the work that we admire. Given certain conditions it appears highly probable that events will happen much as Mr Beresford supposes. The interest is very great. Some of the scenes are highly exciting, nor does Mr Beresford's trained grasp upon the mechanism of behaviour slip or fumble. We feel convinced that a merchant of old Mr Leaming's calibre would continue to mow the field imperturbably under the jeers of the mob. It is he, too, who would be the first to lose his temper at the village council and provoke the leading rebel to shoot him through the head. So far as it goes the psychology is sound and each group of the community is adequately represented by a man or woman of sufficient vitality. But, to tell the truth, the psychology might have been more sketchy than it is without making us uncomfortable. For we are alert to challenge, not the feelings, but the facts. And facts are always disputable. They set one arguing. We find ourselves tempted to suggest alternatives, and seriously wish to draw Mr Beresford's attention to the importance of the cooperative movement which he appears to overlook. Feelings, on the other hand, admit, or should admit, of no dispute. When Mr Beresford introduces Lady Angela and sets her playing Chopin by the light of the last candle we should be convinced that it is Lady Angela who matters, and not the cooperative movement. If our attention wanders it annoys us, because we feel that human beings are too important to be disregarded, and yet, as Lady Angela plays, we cannot help thinking about a possible policy for the left

wing of the Labour Party. We want Mr Beresford to turn
his mind to that problem, directly the Chopin is over. In
short, we want him to give us facts, not fiction.

Postscript or Prelude?

Review of *The Lost Girl*, by D. H. Lawrence.
(2 December, 1920.)

PERHAPS the verdicts of critics would read less preposterously and their opinions would carry greater weight if, in the first place, they bound themselves to declare the standard which they had in mind, and, in the second, confessed the course, bound, in the case of a book read for the first time, to be erratic, by which they reached their final decision. Our standard for Mr Lawrence, then, is a high one. Taking into account the fact, which is so constantly forgotten, that never in the course of the world will there be a second Meredith or a second Hardy, for the sufficient reason that there have already been a Meredith and a Hardy, why, we sometimes asked, should there not be a D. H. Lawrence? By that we meant that we might have to allow him the praise, than which there is none higher, of being himself an original; for such of his work as came our way was disquieting, as the original work of a contemporary writer always is.

This was the standard which we had in mind when we opened *The Lost Girl*. We now go on to trace the strayings and stumblings of that mind as it came to the conclusion that *The Lost Girl* is not an original, or a book which touches the high standard which we have named. Together with our belief in Mr Lawrence's originality went, of course, some sort of forecast as to the direction which that originality was likely to take. We conceived him to be a writer, with an extraordinary sense of the physical world, of the colour and texture and shape of things, for whom the body was alive and the problems of the body insistent and important. It was plain that sex had for him a meaning which it was disquieting to think that we, too, might have to explore. Sex, indeed, was the first red-herring that crossed our path in the new volume. The story is the story of Alvina Houghton, the daughter of a draper in Woodhouse, a mining town in the Midlands. It is all built up of solid fabric. If you want a truthful description of a draper's shop, evident knowledge of his stock, and a faithful and keen yet not satiric or sentimental description of James Houghton, Mrs Houghton, Miss Frost and Miss Pinnegar, here you have it. Nor does this summary do any kind of justice to the variety of the cast and the number of events in which they play their parts. But, distracted by our preconception of what Mr Lawrence was to give us, we turned many pages of very able writing in search for something else which must be there. Alvina seemed the most likely instrument to transmit Mr Lawrence's electric shock through the calicos, prints, and miners' shirts by which she stood surrounded. We watched for signs of her development nervously, for we always dread originality, yet with the sense that once the shock was received we should rise braced and purified. The signs we looked for were not lacking. For example, "Married or unmarried, it was the same—the same anguish, realized in all its pain after the age of fifty—the loss in never having been able to relax, to submit." Again, "She was returning to Woodhouse virgin as she had left it. In a measure she felt herself beaten. Why? Who knows. . . . Fate had been too strong for her and her desires. Fate which was not an external association of forces, but which was integral in her own nature." Such phrases taken in conjunction with the fact that Alvina, having refused her first suitor, wilted and pined, and becoming a midwife mysteriously revived in the atmosphere of the Islington-road, confirmed us in our belief that sex was the magnet to which the myriad of separate details would adhere. We were wrong. Details accumulated; the picture of life in Woodhouse was built up; and sex disappeared. This detail, then this realism, must have another meaning than we had given them. Relieved, yet a trifle disappointed, for we want originality as much as we dread it, we adopted a fresh attitude, and read Mr Lawrence as one reads Mr Bennett—for the facts, and for the story. Mr Lawrence shows indeed something of Mr Bennett's power of displaying by means of immense industry and great ability a section of the hive beneath glass. Like all the other insects, Alvina runs in and out of other people's lives, and it is the pattern of the whole that interests us rather than the fate of one of the individuals.

And then, as we have long ceased to find in reading Mr Bennett, suddenly the method seems to justify itself by a single phrase which we may liken to a glow or to a transparency, since to quote one apart from the context would give no idea of our meaning. In other words, Mr Lawrence occasionally and momentarily achieves that concentration which Tolstoy preserves sometimes for a chapter or more. And then again the laborious process continues of building up a model of life from saying how d'you do, and cutting the loaf, and knocking the cigarette ash into the ash tray, and standing the yellow bicycle against the wall. Little by little Alvina disappears beneath the heap of facts recorded about her, and the only sense in which we feel her to be lost is that we can no longer believe in her existence.

So, though the novel is probably better than any that will appear for the next six months, we are disappointed, and would write Mr Lawrence off as one of the people who have determined to produce seaworthy books were it not for those momentary phrases and for a strong suspicion that the proper way to look at *The Lost Girl* is as a stepping stone in a writer's progress. It is either a postscript or a prelude.